What's Wrong With This House?

A PRACTICAL GUIDE TO FINDING
A WELL DESIGNED SUSTAINABLE HOME

John Brown & Matthew North

Nothing wrong with my
house as long as there
is a Bear, a cow +
a penguin.

My love always
fina
christmas 2011

First published in Canada in 2010
by Slow Home Studio Inc.
202-2212 4 St SW
Calgary, Alberta, Canada T2S 1W9
www.slowhomestudio.com

Second Edition
Copyright © 2011 by John Brown and Matthew North

2011 / 4

Distributed in Canada by Slow Home Studio Inc., Calgary

Printed in Canada

Printed on recycled paper

Library and Archives Canada Cataloguing in Publication
Brown, John and North, Matthew
What's Wrong With This House? / John Brown and Matthew North
Includes index.
ISBN-13: 978-0-9865800-1-7

Slow Home is a Trademark owned by Exhibit A Ltd.

ACKNOWLEDGEMENTS

Matthew and I would like to thank the many people who contributed to this project. First and foremost is our partner, Carina van Olm, whose active involvement in the broader political and social dimensions of the Slow Home philosophy formed the context in which this book exists. Second are all of the Housebrand clients with whom the three of us have worked. Through their projects they generously gave us the opportunity to refine our understanding of good residential design. Finally, we would like to acknowledge Alex Brown for her insight and guidance, Kate Zimmerman for her editorial assistance, and Travis Davidson for his creativity and persistence with the graphic design and production of the book.

John Brown
April, 2011

CONTENTS

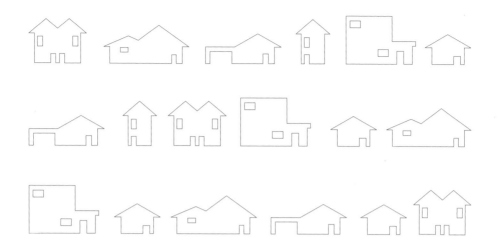

What's Wrong With This House?

A SIMPLE QUESTION

At first glance, *What's Wrong with this House?* might seem like an odd title for a book about residential design. After all, such texts tend to have more positive, uplifting titles that allude to the impossibly perfect lifestyles being portrayed within their pages. We all know the drill: overly glossy images of overly glossy houses; tips, tricks, and trends we know we can't follow; a few hours of decoration daydreaming that frustrate more than fulfill.

This book is different. It focuses on the substance of the way a house works rather than on its superficial appearance. It uses the Slow Home design philosophy to frame a new way of thinking about houses that helps make them simpler to live in and lighter on the environment. This down-to-earth methodology offers practical, relevant design advice for real people looking to make real changes in where and how they live.

The title of this book points to the first step on this journey of change. A physician always begins her work with a diagnostic examination to find out what's wrong with the patient. It is only then that she feels confident prescribing a therapeutic course of action. In the same way, the first step to improving the quality of any residential situation must start with a diagnosis of "What's wrong with this house?"

I begin my first meeting with every new client by asking this question, and after asking it many hundreds, if not thousands, of times during 20 years of practicing residential architecture, I think I've heard almost every possible complaint and concern. But beyond the intriguing idiosyncrasies that each person, and home, brings to the design table, I've also noticed that there are more basic problems that seem to recur over and over again in all types of homes, of all styles and ages, and in all types of neighborhoods and price points.

I am always surprised and dismayed, for example, to discover just how many North American houses have spaces such as formal dining and living rooms, that are only rarely, if ever, used. Many also have features such as oversized bathtubs, artisan staircases, and vaulted spaces that their owners don't really want or even like. They have kitchens that are hard to work in, bathrooms that don't have enough storage, living rooms that are difficult to furnish, laundry spaces that conflict with other uses, and bedrooms that are stuffy and dark.

There are too many houses with bathrooms the size of bedrooms and bedrooms the size of closets. I've seen homes that don't get enough sunlight and an equal number that overheat from having too much sun. There are houses that feel too big and a larger number of others that, despite their actual size, feel too small, cramped, and almost claustrophobic.

After repeatedly coming across these problems, not only in my architectural practice but also in my academic research of the broader housing market, I've come to the unfortunate conclusion that bad design runs rampant throughout North America's housing stock. In saying this, it's important to state that I'm not referring to poor workmanship, bad interior decorating, or superficial exterior styling. While these are obviously areas of concern, and, as mentioned earlier, tend to get a substantial degree of coverage in the design press, they're not what I consider to be the most pressing issues for homeowners. Instead, my alarm stems from the significant and pervasive problems I've seen with the most basic fundamentals of house design.

I'm concerned with how effectively a house functions and how well it suits the ways we want to live. Like wearing a pair of ill-fitting shoes, living in a poorly designed house is uncomfortable and makes the daily routines of life more difficult than they need to be. More often than not, and despite how much we might like the way the shoes or the house look, our enthusiasm fades soon after the purchase. While badly designed shoes can simply be relegated to the back of our closets, a badly designed house is not so easy to dismiss. In most cases, it requires selling up and buying a new home. In fact, dissatisfaction with the way a house functions is one of the primary reasons that people give when buying another home. Over the past ten years, such discontentment has also caused almost 20% of homebuyers to change their mind and move within the first three years of their purchase.[1]

In most cases, this dissatisfaction drives them into buying bigger and more expensive houses. This is certainly good business for the homebuilders, realtors, developers, and banks that make up the residential industry. However, in many situations a move like this doesn't solve the homeowner's dissatisfaction because their new house probably has the same sorts of problems as their old one.

But profound functional flaws are not the only answer to the question of "What's wrong with this house?" From my research as an Architecture Professor in the Faculty of Environmental

---

1   National Association of Realtors, Profile of Home Buyers and Sellers 2007, p. 77-78.

Design at the University of Calgary, I also know that there are issues that extend beyond the individual homeowner. In fact, functional concerns are just the beginning of the problems in North America's housing market. In many ways, our homes also cause us to consume too much energy and generate too high a volume of greenhouse gases.

The typical North American house has an excessively large environmental footprint. In total, building and operating our houses accounts for 70 percent of the nation's electricity consumption, 35 percent of greenhouse gas emissions, and 30 percent of landfill waste.[2] This is in addition to the significant environmental costs associated with all the commuting that most of us have to do each day to get to and from these houses. Even putting aside for a moment the significant ethical issues associated with having such a large environmental impact, the real possibility of much higher fossil fuel costs and some form of future carbon tax will quickly make the majority of our houses unaffordable to operate. We need to seriously question the kind of future that is being created by the houses that are being built today.

Finally, since 2008, the dramatic drop in house prices has overshadowed both the functional and environmental problems with North American housing. For the moment, at least, the most common response to the question of "What's wrong with this house?" is that it has lost so much of its value. To date, $6 trillion of housing wealth has been lost since 2005. Dean Baker, co-director of Washington, D.C.'s Center for Economic Policy Research, estimates that it will take 20 years to recoup the loss.[3] I agree with the experts who believe that, after adjusting for inflation, values may never catch up.

Steadily rising prices in the residential real estate market over the last several decades fooled many people into believing that every house would always increase in value. For a long time, it seemed that almost anything that was built would sell, and then sell over and over again, for ever-larger profits. The result is that too many houses ended up with a value that was based more on financial speculation than on long-term worth. When the market collapsed and buyers disappeared, most of this speculative value also evaporated. These houses lost more value more quickly than houses with strong fundamental worth. They will also be the very last houses to recover their value as the market improves.

---

2   David Suzuki and David R. Boyd, *David Suzuki's Green Guide*, Vancouver: Greystone Books, 2008, p. 21.

3   David Streitfeld, *Housing Fades as a Means to Build Wealth, Analysts Say*, New York Times, Aug. 22, 2010.

OF FOOD AND HOMES

I believe that these functional, environmental and financial responses to the question of "What's wrong with this house?" are not isolated, disconnected problems as much as they are symptoms of a broader dysfunctional relationship that has developed between the housing industry, the homes it produces, and us, the people who live in them.

In many ways, these problems echo the challenges we currently face with the industrialized food industry. Both the food we eat and the places in which we live have profound effects on our emotional, as well as our physical, wellbeing. Historically, our connection with our food and our houses has been deep and intimate, reflecting our relationship with the particular climate and culture in which we live, and our personal and collective histories. Our food and our homes serve to ground us in a rich geographic, historic, and cultural context and give us a much-needed sense of rootedness and connectedness.

This all started to change in the 1940s, when the home-cooked meal made from natural, locally grown ingredients gradually began to be replaced by standardized, processed, "fast" food. At the same time, modest, well-designed homes in walkable neighborhoods started to be replaced by a sprawl of standardized cookie-cutter suburban houses. The shallow relationships that we have with both of these industrialized substitutes erodes the quality of our lives, contributes to a giant ecological footprint, and creates a culture of excess that has little long-term value. This change from the deep relationships we used to have with our food and homes to our current, shallow relationships has transformed us from active, involved producers of our food and homes into lazy, passive consumers of the latest marketing ploy.

The fast food industry promised to make our lives better by making our daily meals easier. But the time saved in the kitchen has come at an even bigger cost to the quality of what we're eating, to say nothing of the high environmental impact of producing and transporting these products around the globe.

The mass production housing industry also promised a better way of life by making our houses bigger and fancier than ever before. In the end, this supersizing has done little to make our lives function any better or our families feel any happier. None of this stuff satisfies the longing we have for a real sense of home.

Sixty years after Richard and Maurice McDonald created the first fast food restaurant in Southern California, and William Levitt introduced the first mass-produced suburb in Levittown, Pennsylvania, we find ourselves in a situation that no one had expected. The fast food industry has unraveled the deeper cultural context of cooking and dining to create an epidemic of obesity and early onset diabetes, as well as a dangerously fragile dependence on globally transported processed food. At the same time, the housing industry has transformed the most important place in our lives into a standardized commodity produced for the lowest possible cost and sold to us for the highest possible price.

The sad reality is that the vast majority of our houses are not even designed by a professional. It's estimated that less than 5 percent of houses in North America have an architect involved in their design and construction. Instead they are designed, to use the term loosely, by drafting technicians, contractors, developers, and marketers who possess little, if any, formal architectural training. Design in this context typically becomes little more than a quick means to a quick end, which is the sale of the house for a big profit. The creation of a high-quality environment in which to live comfortably becomes, at best, an afterthought.

Unfortunately, the multi-billion dollar residential industry that's responsible for almost every house in North America does not seem to be as concerned as it should be with maximizing the functionality, spatial efficiency, quality of life, environmental sustainability, or even long-term value of the houses it's designing and building. Like all sales-driven industries whose primary interest is to sell its product in the shortest possible time and for the biggest possible profit, the residential industry often makes smart design play second fiddle to designs that are easy to market. Whatever helps make the sale is good for business, regardless of whether or not these decisions actually result in a good home. In this situation, the fundamentals of residential design are too easily, and too often, usurped by marketing gimmicks. In fact, this industry cynically relies on our "after the purchase" dissatisfaction with the houses it creates in order to drive future sales.

At its worst, this situation produces what I call "fast houses." Like fast food, these houses are standardized, homogenized commodities that are designed to maximize short-term profits for the industry that creates them, with little regard for the long-term costs to our health and well-being. They also ignore the needs of the broader environment. Fast houses are designed to attract our attention, ignite our desire, and give the illusion of value as much as, if not more than, they are designed to function efficiently as places to live. This means that certain design features in these houses are exploited or exaggerated for marketing effect, while other more basic design fundamentals are ignored or forgotten.

The result is that fast houses make our already busy lives more difficult than they otherwise need to be. They generate more greenhouse gas emissions and consume more energy, water, and other natural resources than they should. In a difficult real estate market, a fast house tends to lose more of its value more quickly than other houses, and it can even more quickly end up not being worth the money that was paid for it.

I want to clarify that the criticisms in this book are about the housing industry as a system of practice and do not extend to the people who work within it. In my long experience in practice I have never met anyone who sets out to intentionally design or build a bad house. Rather, the problems stem from the complex, well entrenched, but now outdated and out of control industrial system in which these people work.

A Slow Home is the antithesis of a fast house. "Slow" is the term I use to describe a home that has been designed to be more personally satisfying, environmentally responsible, and economically reasonable than a fast house. It's like "Slow Food," the name of the movement that arose as a critical alternative to fast food's assault on what and how we eat. In the same way that the Slow Food movement is about paying more attention to where our food comes from and how it's prepared, the Slow Home philosophy is about putting more care and thought into the way our houses are designed.

Put simply, a Slow Home is a well-designed house. It's a house that fits the way we really want to live, and makes the daily rituals of cooking, dining, living, bathing, and sleeping easier and more fulfilling. It has well-proportioned spaces that work the way they're supposed to, are filled with natural light, and have a strong connection to the outdoors. A Slow Home meets these individual needs without jeopardizing the health of the planet. It helps us to minimize our greenhouse gas emissions and substantially reduce our resource consumption. As a result of the attention paid to these critical design issues, a Slow Home is one whose worth is not defined by speculation and real estate bubbles, but by the fundamentals of real value that emerge when a property is a good place to live rather than just a financial play.

The challenge is that, on the surface at least, a fast house and a Slow Home often look very much the same. They can be in the same neighborhood and have a similar price tag. They can be the same size, type, style, and age and have the same interior finishes and detailing. That's because the difference between fast and Slow is not defined by these superficial issues but by the fundamental differences between how these houses work and feel as well as the impact that they have on the environment.

I use fast and Slow as shorthand terms for describing the quality of the design underlying a house. By this, I mean the fundamental organizational decisions that define where the house is located, how well it responds to its context, how efficiently the rooms are organized together, and how effectively each individual space functions. In a fast house, this fundamental structure is flawed and carelessly designed. It results in a house that is awkward to use and environmentally wasteful. A Slow Home, on the other hand, has a logical, thoughtfully designed underlying organizational structure that helps to make our lives easier and reduce our environmental impact.

To date, it has been difficult for people to factor this consideration of design quality into the way they think about their homes. Instead, most people just "drive till they qualify," going further and further out of the city, on the interstate, until they find a house they can afford. The result is that most people end up making one of the most significant decisions of their lives equipped with little more than a vague dream of home and a few overly simplistic real estate metrics, such as floor area, lot width, and a count of bedrooms and baths. Design, when it's considered at all, is usually reduced to decorative issues such as finishes, furniture, colors and the brand name of the fixtures and appliances. While important, these kinds of issues are only worth considering when the fundamentals of the design underlying the house are sound. Moreover, in a world of limited time and attention spans, this focusing on the superficial design of the surface rather than on the fundamental substance of the way the house works actually serves the interests of the fast housing industry. It distracts us from noticing the home's underlying problems until after we've made our purchase and it's too late to change.

Is it any wonder that with this kind of brisk, surface-based house-buying process, so many people end up living in badly designed fast houses?

AN ALTERNATE VISION

For the past 25 years, I've been exploring the many dimensions of this situation through my academic research. I've studied the history of residential development in North America and the business practices of the developers, housebuilding companies, realtors, and mortgage lenders that make it happen. I've analyzed floor plans and feature sheets from across the country to try and understand the logic behind the design decisions in typical fast houses. I've visited scores of model homes, show suites, streets of dreams, and demonstration centers to study common sales practices and compare them to the strategies that other industries use to sell their product. Finally, I've investigated the architecture profession and why it's not more involved in the residential sector of the construction industry.

Twelve years ago, I decided to put this research into practice. Together with my partners, Matthew North and Carina van Olm, I founded Housebrand, a multi-disciplinary architecture firm tailored to the residential market. Our goal was to offer a critical, affordable, and design-centered alternative to the normative housing industry. Quite simply, we wanted to create a firm that could help people across a broad spectrum of housing types and price ranges make better, smarter choices about where and how they should live.

To do this, Matthew and I augmented our architectural training with real estate licenses in order to help our clients with the first design decision they need to make—namely, which property they should buy. To more completely realize our architectural designs, we expanded our firm to include construction services. Finally, after being dissatisfied with the lack of environmentally appropriate furniture and finishing options available in our city, we expanded our company once more with interior design services and a retail design store.

The result is a practice that integrates real estate brokerage, architectural design, construction management, interior design and furniture retailing into a one-stop shop for people looking for an alternative to the typical fast house.

Through Housebrand's unique business model, we've helped hundreds of people to live in Slow Homes. About one third of our projects involve building a new home on an existing lot in an established community. Another third involve remodeling a poorly designed fast house into a better, slower place to live. The final third of our projects utilize our design expertise at a real estate level to help people find an existing Slow Home to purchase.

By its very nature, Housebrand is an intensely local practice, specifically tailored to the city in which it operates, and we have steadfastly resisted the many requests to expand our business to other cities. We felt that this would endanger the slow philosophy on which the firm was founded and engulf us in a fast world mindset of franchises and profit centers.

Instead, four years ago Carina, Matthew, and I started the Slow Home Movement as a way to reach out to a larger audience. For inspiration, we looked to the precedent of the Slow Food Movement's combination of advocacy and public education as a way to help empower individuals to start making better choices in their lives. Through our web-based Slow Home Studio, we translated our professional expertise into common sense, understandable, and relevant design education programs for homeowners.

To increase awareness of the problems with fast houses, and to better understand the dimensions of the fast house problem, we enlisted our rapidly growing online community to participate in a mass collaboration project. Over a nine-month period in 2010, the group analyzed the designs of more than 4,600 new apartment/lofts, townhouses, and single family houses in nine different cities. The result is the first-ever survey of design quality in the North American housing industry.[4] A summary of the key findings can be found in the final chapter of this book.

This combination of academic, professional, and advocacy experiences has convinced Matthew and me that it's possible for people to reevaluate the way they think about their houses and bring them into better alignment with their broader needs and goals. It's possible for everyone to start living in houses that actually function properly as places to eat, sleep, and play.

We believe that it's time to recognize the negative impact our homes are having on the environment and begin to effect real change that will reduce our ecological footprint. It's also time to recognize the new normal of the real estate market and shift our priorities away from the house as a speculative financial vehicle and back to the idea of it as a meaningful place in which to live.

---

4   John Brown & Matthew North, *2010 Slow Home Report on Design Quality in the North American New Home Market*, Calgary: Slow Home Studio, 2011. A digital copy of the report is available at www.slowhomestudio.com

We don't think that anyone really wants to live in a marketing brochure's idea of the good life. No one wants to jeopardize the quality of their children's future by ignoring the environmental impact of our current way of life. And no one wants to spend their hard-earned money on a house that doesn't satisfy their deep emotional need for home.

What follows is an alternate approach that will show you how to make smarter and more environmentally appropriate choices about your home and improve the quality of where and how you live.

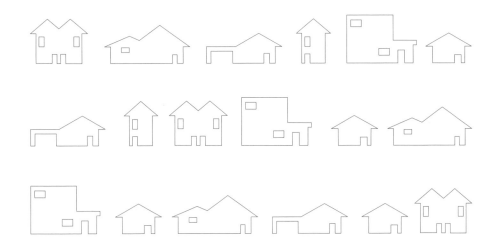

The Story of Tom & Sarah

FAST FOOD — FAST HOUSES

Sarah, Tom, and their one-year-old son Noah were sitting in my office. They had made an appointment to discuss an addition to their 2,450 square foot three bedroom home.

"It's just too small," Sarah said. "Two people can't work in the kitchen, there's too much clutter at the front and back doors, and the family room isn't even big enough for our furniture."

Tom nodded. "Sarah's right. I know it sounds weird but our house feels crowded. I think we really underestimated how much space we would need with a new baby. We definitely need a bigger house."

It was too bad, Sarah said – she and Tom had thought they'd built the perfect home. It had seemed to have everything they were looking for, including a gourmet kitchen upgrade with seven appliances and granite countertops.

Sarah had called me several days earlier to inquire about adding on to their house. She told me that they had built it a little over four years before with one of the large house-building companies. It was located in a new subdivision on the southern outskirts of the city. I learned that she worked as a lawyer for a large manufacturing company. Her husband Tom was an IT consultant and a stay-at-home dad, doing freelance work until Noah was old enough for school.

I had asked the couple to bring along the floor plans of their house. After studying them for a few minutes, I could understand why they were so frustrated with the way their house was working, but I could also see that it had nothing to do with its size. If anything, their house was too big.

"Before we start talking about your addition, let's take a few minutes to analyze the plans so that I can better understand what's wrong with this house," I said.

I began by asking them why they had selected this particular house plan.

Tom replied immediately. "I really liked the staircase at the front door. It looked cool and different."

TOM & SARAH'S HOUSE

Main Floor
Interior - 1150 ft²
Garage - 425 ft²

Upper Floor
Interior -1300 ft²

Taking out my red pen, I started my analysis. "That's very interesting," I said. "It seems to me that one of the big things wrong with the inside of this house is that stair. Notice how it's rotated on a 45-degree angle to the main walls in the house. While that makes it more noticeable when you first walk in, look at what effect it has on the kitchen. The counter and the island are angled to match the stair in order for there to be enough room to move around, but notice how those angled counters make it more difficult to work in the kitchen. I think that's why you find it so cramped. It isn't the size as much as it is the layout that's making it awkward to use. And all those extra appliances take up too much space, which just makes a bad situation worse."

"So that's why the eating bar feels too small," Sarah said. "That's another thing that really frustrates me about this house."

Tom said they'd bought the gourmet kitchen upgrade because he'd wanted to learn how to cook. As it turned out, the couple was too busy to do anything more in terms of cooking than the basics. Meanwhile, he confessed that he no longer even noticed the stair that lured him into the house in the first place.

"The problem with the geometry of the stair also explains why your family room feels small," I said. "Notice how the side wall and fireplace in that room are at the same angle as the stair but that the other two walls follow the geometry of the rest of the house. This collision of geometries makes this room difficult to use because you don't know which direction the furniture should face. It's like putting a square peg in a round hole — no matter what you do, there's always going to be a lot of wasted space."

"I never really liked that stair, I just didn't know why," Sarah said with a smile. "But from my point of view, I remember wanting this house because we could have a formal sitting and dining room, as well as informal areas for the family. That was something we had never had before and it made it feel like a real family house."

"That's interesting," I said. "How often do you use that formal living room?"

"Never," said Tom. "The furniture in there is just some old stuff that we inherited from Sarah's grandmother."

"And the dining room?" I asked.

"Well, we've probably had two Thanksgiving dinners with Tom's family since we moved in and another couple of dinner parties with some friends before Noah came along. Other than that, we hardly ever go in there," Sarah replied.

"Looking at the floor plan again, we can see that the formal living and dining rooms take up about one quarter of the main floor," I said. "But from what you're telling me, you hardly ever use them. That means the effective size of the main floor, the space that you actually use on a daily basis, is closer to 950 than 1,150 square feet. That's a pretty big difference, particularly when you consider that the family room and the kitchen, the two rooms you spend most of your time in, are actually difficult to use because of their shape."

"You're right. No wonder the house feels small," said Tom, with a frustrated look on his face.

"So where do you eat most of your meals?" I asked.

"At the round table in the breakfast nook," replied Tom.

"It doesn't look like there's much room back there. I'll bet that table is a bit small for a family of three," I observed. "Plus, I see that the door to the backyard is right there. That must be awkward when you want to go outside."

"Yeah, the door swings in and hits the table," Sarah said. "It's really annoying."

I next asked Sarah and Tom about where they kept their coats and boots. "We have coat hooks on the wall in the laundry room and the boots just stay by the front and back doors. But ever since the baby arrived, the back area is always clogged up with laundry so we now use the front door most of the time. We usually end up just dropping everything on the floor inside the door. The mess really drives me crazy," said Sarah.

"Let's look at the plan again," I said. "It's pretty clear to me that the back entry is too small to do double duty as a laundry room. Notice how you have to pass right in front of the machines to get to and from the garage. That floor space will always be filled with your laundry basket and it really shouldn't be a main thoroughfare. The second problem is that there's no front entry space. Notice how the front door opens directly into the living room, so you will always see whatever is left on the floor. Plus, with no front closet, I don't think anybody could keep it neat and tidy."

"See!" Tom said to Sarah, laughing. "It isn't my fault that the house is a mess when you come home."

Finishing off my analysis of the main floor, I asked about the guest bathroom. Sarah said nobody used it because the door opened directly into the family room. She and Tom told guests to go upstairs and use the family bathroom.

MAIN FLOOR ANALYSIS

1   Over-sized angled stair disrupts circulation from foyer to family room.

2   Angled counters make the kitchen difficult to work in.

3   Unnecessary kitchen appliances take up too much space.

4   Eating bar is too short.

5   Breakfast nook is too small and table location conflicts with door swing.

6   Corner fireplace in family room causes inefficient diagonal furniture layout.

7   Guest bathroom door opens directly into family room.

8   Circulation conflict with laundry in back entry.

9   Foyer has no closet and opens directly into living room.

10   Formal living and dining rooms are seldom used.

11   Side yard window in formal dining room does not provide sufficient daylight.

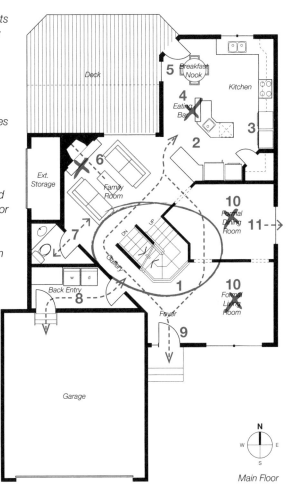

Main Floor

"I understand the concern about the guest bath's location," I said, "but I also worry about the shape of the room. It must be awkward having the sink in the corner like that. How does the mirror work?"

"Don't ask," Tom said. "That was one of the nasty shocks we had when we moved in. I didn't think to look in the guest bathroom of the model house when we were going through the purchase process. Why would anyone put a sink in the corner like that?"

Politely ignoring the question, I suggested that we move on to the second floor. Unfortunately, a quick glance at the floor plan told me that the situation was little better upstairs. The rotated stair was just as disruptive on this level, resulting in nonfunctional triangular closets, oddly shaped bedrooms, and an excessive amount of circulation space for a house of this size.

"Interesting study loft," I said. "Do you use it much?"

"It's silly," Sarah replied. "It's right at the top of the stairs and beside the bathroom. No one has ever sat there to work. It's just a place that gathers junk!"

"The same is true of the library," added Tom. "We were excited about owning a home with a real library but it turns out to be a useless space. It's too long and narrow and has only one small window. I tried working there but after a couple of months, I gave up and moved my office into the third bedroom. That turned into a real problem when Sarah's parents were visiting."

"Speaking of the bedrooms," I said, "the second bedroom is a very strange shape and hardly looks big enough to hold a bed. I'll bet the door swing must come very close to hitting the end of the frame. The third bedroom, the one you're using as an office, is a better size and shape but it only has a side yard window. You must just look out onto the blank wall of your neighbor's house. That room probably doesn't get much sunlight. Finally, the master bedroom and en-suite bathroom are disproportionately large compared to the rest of the house. It would have been better if some of that space had been devoted to making the other rooms more functional."

UPPER FLOOR ANALYSIS

1   Angled stair creates awkward triangular hall closet.

2   Door swing conflicts with bed placement in bedroom 2.

3   Angled stair reduces closet length in bedroom 2.

4   Angled stair creates excessive hallway circulation to library.

5   Awkwardly placed study desk adjacent to bathroom door.

6   Library is too long and narrow with an insufficiently sized window.

7   Window in bedroom 3 faces side yard and has limited daylight.

8   Master bedroom is over-sized and has wasted space.

9   Master en-suite is inefficient with too much floor space.

10 Vanity cabinet has two sinks but no storage.

11 Toilet is awkwardly located adjacent to walk-in closet door.

12 Walk-in closet has excessive floor area and insufficient hanging space.

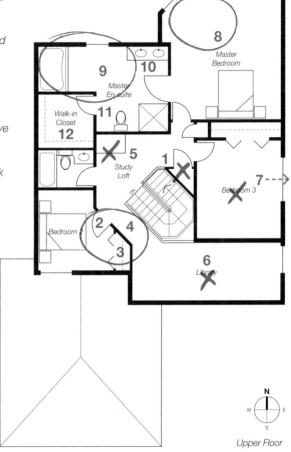

Upper Floor

Sarah said that the over-sized master bedroom was another of her pet peeves. While it was handy for Noah's crib when he was a baby, now that he had graduated to his own room, the extra floor area in the master bedroom was just a repository for Tom's sports equipment and two rolling racks of her clothes.

"That's another problem," Tom added. "Our closet is way too small for two people. We thought it looked big in the show home but there weren't any clothes in it then."

Turning to the bathrooms, I said, "The family bathroom seems to be okay except for the lack of storage space. That will be an issue if you have more kids. But I'm more concerned with the master bathroom."

The floor area in this room was large—in fact, it was almost the size of one of the secondary bedrooms. The layout, however, was bad. It was clear to me that this was a room that would only be impressive at first glance. The toilet was awkwardly located on a side wall that was inconveniently close to the closet, the stand-alone shower was quite small and situated behind the door, and the sink counter was short, despite the fact that it contained two sinks. The primary feature of this en-suite was a lot of wasted space in the middle of the room.

I asked Sarah where she stored her hair dryer.

"Ha! That's a good question," she replied. "You've noticed that there's no storage in our vanity. We didn't realize that until the first night we slept in our new house. The en-suite in the model house looked fabulous. It seemed luxurious and I think they call it a 'spa bath' in the brochure. But when we moved in and I went to put away our toiletries, bingo—no storage. What a surprise."

I had noticed on the brochure that an eco-package upgrade had been available, and I asked Tom and Sarah if they had added it to their home.

"Of course," said Tom proudly. "We're both really concerned about the environment. Plus, when you have kids it makes you think about the future. Noah needs to have a world with lots of clean water and air. "

In looking over the details of the package, I could see that it included a short list of usual sustainable products and energy-saving equipment. While it certainly helped for Tom and Sarah's house to have these features, they probably wouldn't have much impact on the size of the house's environmental footprint. From a sustainable point of view, the house had bigger problems.

"Let's talk about your lot," I said. "You chose it yourself, right?"

"You bet," Tom enthusiastically replied. "We were really lucky. There was only one oversized loft left when we went to the showroom, so we snatched it up right away before anyone else could get it."

I could see from the floor plan that the lot Tom and Sarah had been so excited about was oriented so that the front of the house faced south.

"Lot size is certainly a consideration, but from an environmental point of view, I don't think it was such a great choice," I said. "The solar orientation of the lot doesn't match the house plan very well."

All of the principal living spaces in this house, as well as the master bedroom, looked out to the backyard. On the lot they selected, that backyard faced north. As a result, the principal rooms got little sunlight. The south side of the house, which was bathed in natural light most of the day, primarily consisted of the garage. The result was that the only south light to enter the house was through the window in the formal living room that was rarely used, and the awkwardly shaped second bedroom. In a cold climate, this was a missed opportunity to naturally heat the house and reduce its energy load.

"The lot you chose restricts the ability of your house to take advantage of the sun's free energy to provide natural light and heat to the interior. In the end, this means that your house is going to require more energy, and that boosts the size of your environmental footprint. Plus, I bet the house feels a little gloomy inside, no matter how nice a day it is."

I concluded our meeting with a final question. "How long is your commute?"

ORIENTATION ANALYSIS

This house does not have good solar orientation for the cold climate in which it is located.

1. *The east facing formal dining room will receive limited morning light because the window faces into a side yard.*

2. *The south facing formal living room has the best solar orientation, but this room is seldom used.*

3. *The double attached garage faces south, but requires no daylighting.*

4. *Most of the windows of the principal spaces face north and as a result the interior will get very little direct sunlight.*

Tom said that as a telecommuter, he only had to go upstairs at the moment, but when he returned to his job he'd have a 15-minute drive each way. Sarah, on the other hand, worked at the other end of the city, and spent about 90 minutes in the car, driving to and from work, each day. This was a big problem. Motor vehicles are the single biggest source of atmospheric pollution, contributing an estimated 14 percent of the world's carbon dioxide emissions from fossil fuel burning. The typical car produces 300 pounds of CO2/ tank of gasoline.[5] Assuming that Sarah needed to fill up her car with gas once a week, her driving generated almost 15,000 pounds of CO2 annually. That was almost as much as the 18,000 pounds of CO2 that a typical two-person home generates per year.[6]

"I think being located so far from where you work is probably one of the biggest problems with your house," I said. "The environmental impact of all that commuting is just too great. Plus there's the time factor. Sarah, did you realize that you are spending the equivalent of almost one full work-day per week in your car? That's time you should be spending with Tom and your son."

"I never thought of it like that before," Sarah said glumly. "We picked our neighborhood because the house prices were affordable. It seems like a false economy now."

The combination of poor solar orientation and long automobile commutes made for crucial environmental shortcomings in this house. They far outweighed the more piece-meal environmental benefits of the products in the eco-package upgrade that the couple had added when they made their purchase.

As I put down my red pen, Tom looked defeated and Sarah looked upset. They had both come to the realization that they had purchased the wrong house.

"Don't be too discouraged," I said. "Yours is certainly not the worst house I've ever seen. Let's get together again in a few days and talk about your options."

As they were leaving the office, I suggested that we have our next meeting at their house.

---

5   http://www.worldcarfree.net/resources/stats.php#1, Accessed Feb. 2011
6   http://www.epa.gov/climatechange/emissions/ind_home.html, Accessed Feb. 2011

DESIGNED-TO-BE-SOLD

Like many of us, this young couple is caught in a dilemma. They have a busy life and are trying to make their way in a complex world. They want a home that will make their daily routines easier and their family life richer. As an investment, they want their home to build financial security for the future. These are reasonable and important expectations that all of us should have for our houses. As so commonly happens, however, the reality of what Tom and Sarah ended up with bears little resemblance to these original goals.

Their house is difficult to live in. It feels small and cramped, even though it has several spaces that rarely get used. It has features they paid a lot of money for but don't really like. The house has a big environmental footprint due to the amount of commuting that's required and the high energy cost of operating an inefficiently designed and improperly sited house. Any increase in the price of energy will also have a significant impact on their monthly budget. At the same time, like many people across the country, Tom and Sarah have seen the value of their house decline significantly in recent years. Current trends indicate that in this economic recession, standardized new suburban houses like Tom and Sarah's have generally suffered greater instability in value than older homes in more central, established communities. As the situation begins to improve, this segment of the market also appears to be taking longer to recover.

Tom and Sarah's dilemma is the result of a series of unfortunate choices that led them to buy the wrong kind of house. They made these choices with the best intentions but the result was not what they expected.

Their house-buying process started innocently enough. Like many of their friends, and their parents before them, the couple purchased a house that was designed and built by a large company. All the houses in their neighborhood were constructed by this company, using four of its standard floor plans. Tom and Sarah toured all the model homes and visited the builder's showroom to choose a lot. They went to the company's design center to select their colors and floor finishes and choose from a limited series of upgrade packages. They selected the house plan, lot, and upgrades that were the right combination of size and price, and arranged their financing with the onsite mortgage company. The whole process was completed in less than a week, and they moved into their new house about 90 days later.

Tom and Sarah live in what we call a fast house.

THE HIGH COST OF COMMUTING

Oregon-based economist Joe Cortright argues that the increasing cost of gasoline is having a significant impact on the long term economic value of our houses. In a recently published study of the American housing market entitled Driven to the Brink—How the Gas Price Spike Popped the Housing Bubble and Devalued the Suburbs he states,

"The collapse of America's housing bubble—and its reverberations in financial markets—have obscured a tectonic shift in housing demand. Although housing prices are in decline almost everywhere, price declines are generally far more severe in far-flung suburbs and in metropolitan areas with weak close-in neighborhoods. The reason for this shift is rooted in the dramatic increase in gas prices over the past five years. Housing in cities and neighborhoods that require lengthy commutes and provide few transportation alternatives to the private vehicle are falling in value more precipitously than in more central, compact and accessible places."[†]

The reason for this shift is that the suburban model of development favored by the fast housing industry requires not only a consistent supply of land for new lots but a ready supply of cheap gas for commuting. According to Cortright, the run up in gas prices has rewritten the fundamentals of suburban housing economics as people become less willing to buy houses that require more driving.

"The better accessibility provided by dense, close-in urban neighborhoods is reflected in housing markets. Houses with these attributes command higher prices. Controlling for house size, lot size, school quality and other neighborhood characteristics, a house 1 mile closer to the center of Austin, Texas, was worth $8,000 more than a house 1 mile farther away. Plus, each minute shaved off average commute times increased a house's value by $4,700."

The clear conclusion is that the purchasing strategy of "driving till you qualify" promoted by the fast housing industry is quickly becoming irrelevant. In the medium to long term, houses located a great distance from employment centers and other kinds of civic amenities are in substantial danger of losing economic value.

---

† 　J. Cortright, *Driven to the Brink*, Portland: Connections, 2008.

It's one of almost 500 nearly identical single family houses located on a series of nearly identical gently curving streets in one of a dozen nearly identical neighborhoods currently being developed on the outskirts of the city. These cookie-cutter houses are like fast food—standardized, repetitive, monotonous, and anonymously produced. They are fast houses produced by a fast housing industry composed of large land development companies, national home-builders, multi-national real estate franchises, and large financial institutions. But fast houses are not just found in suburban sprawl. They exist in the inner city as well as in suburbia. They can be new townhouses or low-high rise apartments, just as easily as single-family homes. Nor are fast houses always new. The fast housing industry has been building this way for the past 60 years and older fast houses can be found throughout many established communities. Finally, cost is not even a determining factor, because fast houses are found across the spectrum of the market, from modestly priced to expensive.

Given this diversity, what defining characteristic do all these houses share? What makes Tom and Sarah's house, and all the other fast houses, so difficult to live in, hard on the environment, and, in most cases, not worth all of the money that was paid for them? What, in essence, is a fast house?

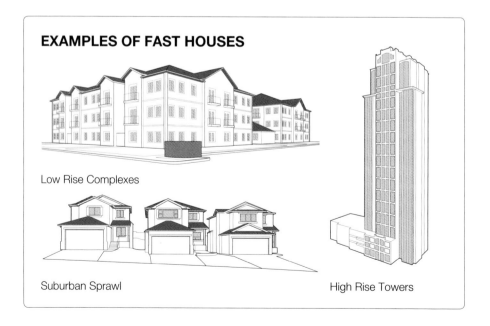

EXAMPLES OF FAST HOUSES

Low Rise Complexes

Suburban Sprawl

High Rise Towers

The simple answer is that a fast house is one that has been designed to be sold.

By this, I mean that many of the basic design elements in the house have been intentionally manipulated by the homebuilding industry to make it appear more attractive to a potential buyer.

Like handbags and hamburgers, these houses have been reduced to mass-produced commodities overlaid with sophisticated marketing tactics that seduce us into making the purchase. While this certainly generates more profits for the fast housing industry, in most cases, unfortunately, it also results in houses that don't function as well as they should. The reason is that most of the design/marketing strategies that make a house compelling at the time of sale are not necessarily beneficial in the long run. In fact, they can often cause significant problems in the way a house functions on a day-to-day basis. At the same time, the focus on designing for sale instead of for use means that many of the fundamental principles of good residential design are either forgotten or ignored.

The situation is similar to the problem with fast food, which is also intentionally manipulated to make us want to purchase it. Does anyone still think that processed food exists to satisfy our biological need for nourishment?

In *The End of Overeating*, David A. Kessler, a former commissioner of the Food and Drug Administration, describes a food product development expert who is trying to "unlock the code of craveability" in order to intentionally trigger a biological response to overindulge in his company's product. Other consultants describe how they purposefully design food products that offer what's become known as "eatertainment," with high quantities of salt, fat, and sugar.[7] It doesn't matter to the fast food industry that this designed-to-be-sold attitude means it is making products that are bad for us.

A simple hamburger, for instance, is no longer enough on its own. It needs to be supersized, with triple the cheese, extra bacon, and too much high-fat-content sauce. It has been designed to catch our attention, ignite our desire, and give us the illusion of value rather than to actually nourish our bodies. The long-term impact on our health is not the fast food industry's concern. We buy this kind of food at our own risk.

---

7   David Kessler, *The End of Overeating, Taking Control of the Insatiable American Appetite*, New York: Rodale Books, 2009.

In the Design Quality Survey [8], that Matthew and I completed in 2010, studying the North American housing industry, we discovered that four designed-to-be-sold strategies—colliding geometries, redundant spaces, false labeling, and supersizing—kept recurring in all house types and sizes. They were found across all price ranges and in all nine of the cities that we surveyed. In every case, these strategies negatively impacted the long-term design quality of the house, making it difficult to live in and harder on the environment. We believe that they are employed by the fast house industry for marketing purposes more than to make the house better to live in. In other words, they are designed to catch our attention, ignite our desire, and give us the illusion of value in much the same way that the dramatic photography, juicy description, and supersized ingredient list seduces us into buying a triple cheese bacon burger. Despite the allure of their first impressions, we buy houses that contain these features at our own risk.

COLLIDING GEOMETRIES

The first designed-to-be-sold strategy we identified was the use of colliding geometries to catch our attention when we first walk into a house. They result whenever walls, stairs, kitchen counters, and fireplaces are organized on a 45-degree angle to the orthogonal geometry in the rest of the plan. Our eyes notice things that are different from their surroundings, and advertisers have long used this fact to attract potential buyers. The foreign geometry collides with the rest of the house and makes it stand out and look more dramatic than it really is. However, this strategy can cause significant long-term problems when applied to the design of a home. Dramatic visual devices such as this usually end up fragmenting the spaces in a floor plan, causing serious disruptions to the way the rest of the house works.

In Tom and Sarah's house, the rotated stair is a marketing device as much as it is a way to get upstairs. Walking into the model house for the first time, Tom was struck by how unique the stair made the house look. The angled stair and walls accomplished their task: to make the house stand out and be noticed by a buyer.

---

8   John Brown & Matthew North, *2010 Slow Home Report on Design Quality in the North American New Home Market.* Calgary: Slow Home Studio, 2011.

Unfortunately, and unbeknownst to Sarah and Tom, this collision of geometries also significantly disrupts the functionality of their kitchen and their ability to properly furnish their family room. As we've seen, the day-to-day frustrations of living with these deficiencies remain long after the visual spectacle of the unusually shaped elements has been forgotten.

REDUNDANT SPACES

The use of redundant spaces is the second designed-to-be-sold strategy we identified in our survey. They are employed to ignite our desire by artificially inflating the allure of a home with extra rooms and functions. The fast house industry counts on the fact that most people give very little thought to the usefulness, or even necessity, of these extra spaces at the point of purchase. Unfortunately, the lack of actual value that they provide soon becomes apparent when you move in and realize that these spaces are redundant, difficult to furnish, and perhaps even unpleasant to be in.

In Tom and Sarah's house, the formal living and dining rooms are as much marketing devices as they are places to sit. The names sound grand and they figure prominently in the sales brochure. Their purpose is to promise the buyers something special that they didn't think they could afford. This was obviously successful in Tom and Sarah's case because their presence convinced Sarah that this was the "real family home" that she had always wanted.

The reality, however, is that these spaces are rarely used. They've turned out to be superfluous because Tom and Sarah use the family room and eating nook at the back of the house instead.

Both of the eating spaces in Tom and Sarah's house are poorly designed. The redundant formal dining room is too enclosed and too removed from the family room to be used on a daily basis. The breakfast nook is too small and awkwardly located to be functional. Design deficiencies also exist in the two living spaces. The redundant formal living room is too small and too removed from the main living areas of the house to be well used, and the corner fireplace in the family room makes it difficult to furnish. If the floor area of these redundant spaces had been allocated to making one living space and one dining space that were well designed, Tom and Sarah probably wouldn't feel that their house was too small.

DESIGNED-TO-BE-SOLD STRATEGIES IN TOM & SARAH`S HOUSE

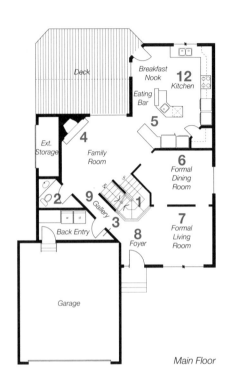

Main Floor

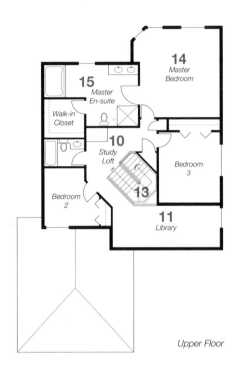

Upper Floor

COLLIDING GEOMETRIES
45 degree angled walls and features

1   Angled stair
2   Triangular guest bathroom
3   Wasted space behind laundry door
4   Corner fireplace
5   Angled kitchen counters and island

REDUNDANT SPACES
Duplicated and unnecessary rooms

6   Underused formal dining room
7   Underused formal living room

FALSE LABELING
Spaces in name only

8   Foyer
9   Gallery
10   Study loft
11   Library

SUPERSIZING
Overscaled floor areas and fixtures

12   Kitchen floor area and appliances
13   Angled stair
14   Master bedroom floor area
15   Master en-suite floor area and
     jacuzzi tub

FALSE LABELING

False labeling is a designed-to-be-sold strategy that makes a house look better in the sales brochure than it is in reality. Its purpose is to ignite desire with the promise of a great feature.

The problem is that false labeling of spaces in a fast house can mask significant design deficiencies that might not become evident until after you have moved in. Perhaps the most common falsely labeled space is the "study" or "home office." In many fast houses, any wasted bit of space can suddenly be defined as a "study" on the floor plan. Too often these spaces are just too small, too dark, or too oddly shaped to function effectively. The practice is particularly common in multi-family projects where the addition of a study will often bump a unit into the next higher price category, regardless of the quality, or even utility, of that space.

In Tom and Sarah's house, the upper floor study loft and library are marketing tools more than they are places to sit and read. The study loft is much too small to be useful. It has no natural light and is too close to both the stair and the bathroom door to actually be a pleasant space to read, work or do anything else. The library is just a small unusable area behind the stair with little natural light. In reality, it's just a storage space.

On the main floor, the gallery and foyer are also falsely labeled spaces. Despite their grandiose names, the gallery is nothing more than an awkward hallway beside the stair and the foyer is only a small bit of tile at the front door.

SUPERSIZING

Supersizing is the final, and perhaps most common, designed-to-be-sold strategy that we identified in our survey. Bloated house sizes, over-sized rooms, and over-scaled fixtures such as bathtubs and staircases are used to give an illusion of value. The intent is to convince us that the house we are considering is just too good a deal to pass up. Supersizing seduces the buyer with the offer of more product at a cut-rate price. In reality, it trades off quality for quantity. In most cases, the functional value of these supersized elements is much less than the more reasonably scaled versions.

Supersizing gives the illusion that we are getting something for next-to-nothing. In fact, the opposite is true. Both fast food producers and fast house builders use supersizing to dramatically increase their profits while adding minimal value to the product they are selling. For example, a supersized order of french fries has essentially the same fixed costs as the normal order, except for a small additional cost for more potatoes. This means that the additional price of the supersized version is almost entirely profit.

The same is true of houses. In a typical supersized house, the additional floor area is usually concentrated in the living areas and bedrooms. The cost of building this additional space is quite low, because the expensive parts of the house, namely the kitchen and bathrooms, are left unchanged, and the fixed costs for land, servicing, stairs, windows, doors, and other major construction components remain the same. The result is that the additional house size commands a much higher sale price that, like the french fries, is almost entirely profit for the home builder.

Tom and Sarah's oversized master bedroom and adjoining bath are more marketing devices than they are places in which to sleep and get ready each morning. Designed-to-be-sold products like these are used to give the illusion of value in order to make the sale. The blissful indulgence promised by an extra-large bedroom and en-suite were simply too much for Tom and Sarah to resist.

In reality, these two rooms are anything but luxurious. The oversized floor area in the master bedroom serves no real purpose. It just makes the room difficult to furnish, with the result that it feels rather empty. The bathroom is also oversized for no practical reason. The extra size results in a large empty space in the middle of the room that does nothing to improve its efficiency or effectiveness. At the same time, two critically important areas of the bathroom are severely undersized. The sink cabinet has no storage and is barely large enough to accommodate two sinks. The shower stall is also a minimal size that's awkward to use. The result is a master bedroom and bathroom that only look good on paper.

We are no match for these sophisticated fast house marketing tactics. In the same way that the fast food industry wants us to focus on the size of the soda cup rather than the amount of sugar in the drink, the fast housing industry also wants us to focus on quantity rather than quality, on marketing rather than design, and on short-term gain rather than long-term value. In this system of evaluation, "bigger" and "more" will always seem better, even if they actually work to our detriment.

As a result, and instead of carefully considering the quality and effectiveness of the design underlying a house, most of us just walk into a model home, or an existing house that is listed for sale, armed with nothing more than the real estate statistics on the one-page listing sheet. In most cases, we have no idea what to look for beyond some vague sense of whether this house "feels right" or not. In fact, many of us spend more time choosing a flat screen television than we do inside a house that we are just about to purchase. Too often, we then end up basing one of our most personally and financially significant decisions on a series of first impressions and ill-defined feelings. These are precisely the areas that the designed-to-be-sold marketing strategies of a fast house manipulate so well. As a result, most of us, quite unwittingly, end up buying fast houses.

When this happens, it usually doesn't take long for things to unravel. As the new homeowner, all the problems that you couldn't see on your pre-sale tour become crystal clear after you move in. The "great room" that caught your eye is actually hard to furnish, the "trophy kitchen" is difficult to use, and the "executive style" walk-in closet is really just a waste of space. You also begin to notice that some of the basics are missing or wrong. These can be really annoying, like a bedroom that can't fit a bed, doors that swing into each other, or a bathroom with two sinks but no storage.

Within a couple of years, your level of dissatisfaction rises to the point where you decide to make a change. You may not know exactly what's wrong with your house, but you certainly know that this one isn't right. The housing industry is quick to tell you that happiness can be found just around the corner, in a bigger and more expensive home. But using the same old process for choosing your next house frequently results in a purchase that has many, if not all, of the same design flaws as your old one. And so the cycle continues, each time generating ever more greenhouse gases, depleting ever more natural resources, and costing you ever more time, energy, and money. We've become a nation of serial house buyers, always on the lookout for that elusive feeling of home without really knowing how to go about finding it.

The problems caused by fast food and fast houses, however, extend well beyond the ill effects of the individual hamburger and house. These are just the last, most visible, parts of a much more extensive set of broad environmental consequences. In fast food, for example, the enormous agri-business and transportation systems that support the fast food industry have large environmental effects that include greenhouse gas emissions, oil and water consumption, soil degradation, deforestation, and pollution. The fast food industry doesn't want us to think about this. It works hard to hide its high environmental costs for the same reasons that it masks the vast calorie count of its meals.

Not surprisingly, no one wants to think about the high environmental cost of our houses, either. For the past 60 years, developers have created a seemingly endless sprawl of suburban communities in order to ensure a ready supply of cheap, easy-to-access lots on which they can build. This kind of low-density development has high environmental costs, ranging from the infrastructure of roads, utilities, and other amenities that are required to service these houses, to the greenhouse gases generated by extensive commuting. Typically, these environmental loads far outweigh the benefits of the highly visible, and much touted, "green wash" of products that are now being applied to almost every new fast house. Tom and Sarah are caught up in this situation. They were seduced into buying a cleverly conceived substitute for a home that looked good at first glance but soon turned into a big problem. Their house is the result of a flawed design process that focuses on expediency and short-term thinking at the expense of long-term quality. It was designed-to-be-sold more than it was designed to be lived in. As a result, it makes the daily lives of Tom and Sarah more difficult than they need to be, creates an overly large environmental impact, and jeopardizes the long-term value of their financial investment.

MAKING A CHANGE

"I think we need to move," Sarah said as Matthew and I sat down at the table in their breakfast nook. We had just arrived at Sarah and Tom's house for our second meeting.

"Your analysis last week really hit home. Now, all I can see are problems everywhere I look. Tom still thinks an addition will give us more living space, but, for me, the only answer is to find another place to live."

Matthew responded. "We don't think an addition is a good idea. Your house is already 2,450 square feet. That's a reasonable size for a young family and we don't think that adding more rooms is going to solve your problems. As I understand it, the issues aren't so much with the amount of space you have, but the way in which it's been designed."

"But we also don't think you should be thinking about a move right now, either," I added.

Several years ago, our answer would probably have been different. Prior to the collapse of the housing market, the easiest solution for Tom and Sarah would have been to sell up and buy a better-designed home. But times have changed. The current housing market bears little resemblance to the one that existed when the couple first purchased their house. The 2008 financial crisis has dramatically reduced house values and created a large oversupply of property on the resale market. Like most people, making a move to a different house is probably not something that Tom and Sarah should reasonably consider at this point.

"But we can't take living in our house much longer," Sarah said. "With my promotion, I think we can afford to take a big loss on this house and still buy another place. We've got our savings. That's enough for a good down payment. It won't be easy starting over, though."

"You're fortunate to have that option," I said, "but I still think you should stay in this house. You shouldn't abandon your original equity. Prices will start to go back up, at least somewhat, in the next few years. The longer you can wait it out, the better off you'll be. I think you should plan to stay put for at least another five years."

"But how are we going to do that?" Sarah said, looking worried. "This house just doesn't work for us."

"It may not work right now," Matthew said, with a smile, "but we have some ideas."

I said we thought the best option for Sarah and Tom was a series of modest changes that would fix the most glaring problems with their house. It would be a more moderate and incremental approach than either a move or a big addition.

"Okay," Sarah said hesitantly, "but it seems a bit strange to put even more money into this house."

"We don't think that it will cost all that much to make your house work much better," I explained. "Although it still won't be perfect, it will certainly make it easier for you to live in over the next five years."

"And also easier to sell when the time comes," Matthew added.

"That sounds good to me. Let's see what they're suggesting, honey," Tom said, as he put his arm around a still-skeptical Sarah.

Tom and Sarah's house suffered badly from all four of the afore-mentioned designed-to-be-sold strategies. Our goal was to minimize their negative impact and improve livability without incurring too many costs. We had prepared a set of revised plans and began with a review of the concept design for the main floor.

"To reduce the impact of the colliding geometries, you'll see that we removed the corner fireplace and the angled cabinets and counters in the kitchen," Matthew said. "Let's concentrate on the family room for a minute. Notice that we relocated the fireplace onto the side wall and set it into the storage room to save space."

"Look at what that does to the family room," I pointed out. "The furniture can now be oriented to the outside walls rather than the 45 degree angle fireplace. When the furniture grouping is organized around this new focal point, all of the wasted space in the room is eliminated. This will dramatically increase livability."

"There's actually a lot of space in that room," Tom said, "now that we can make use of all of it."

Turning everyone's attention to the kitchen, Matthew said, "We wouldn't normally consider making changes to a kitchen that's only four years old. However, in this particular situation, the functional problems are so significant that it seemed like making some alterations to the cabinetry was justifiable. In the end, we think making these changes will add more value to the house."

"Makes sense to me," Sarah responded.

"I think I can reuse the cabinets in the garage, anyway," Tom said. "I've been wanting more storage space in there, and a workbench would be great."

REVISING THE FAMILY ROOM, KITCHEN AND DINING ROOM

1 *Fireplace relocated to center of side wall for more effective furniture layout.*

2 *Corner pantry eliminated and excess appliances removed to improve efficiency of kitchen.*

3 *Large three foot deep rectangular island added to create more efficient appliance triangle, additional work surface, storage, and more eating bar seating.*

4 *Elimination of breakfast nook eliminates door swing conflict.*

5 *Dining room walls removed to visually connect formal dining space with family room and kitchen.*

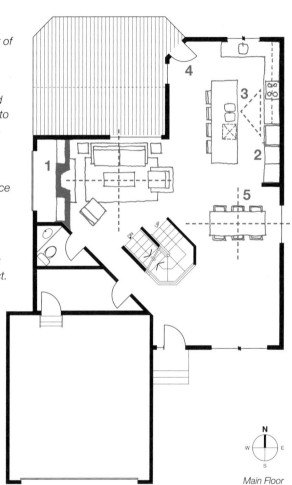

Main Floor

"We suggest removing the corner pantry and relocating the refrigerator and wall ovens," I said. "You'll notice that we removed the angled counter by the family room and replaced the angled island with a longer rectangular version that extends into the breakfast nook."

"We think the house will work much better if the kitchen expands into the nook," Matthew said. "Notice how there is now a much more efficient work triangle between the three primary appliances. There's also more counter space and storage, which will make it easier for you both to work in the kitchen at the same time."

Moving over to the plan for the dining room, Matthew described how we had removed the walls between the dining room, kitchen, and family room to create a more open space for the dining table that was better connected to the rest of the house.

"That makes the house feel bigger," Sarah said. "It'll also be nice to use our dining room table every day. I can see Noah doing his homework in there when he's old enough to go to school."

The third change was to transform the redundant, and largely unused, formal living space at the front of the house into a much more useful office for Tom. We proposed closing off the doorways into the dining room and adding a bookshelf/storage unit across the back wall. We also added a new coat closet to create a separation between the front entry and the study. A desk for Tom faced the window.

"This will be a really great sunlight-filled space in which to work." I said, "It's private, but not too far removed from the main living areas."

"And that closet will take care of all the mess that's there right now," Tom said, with a smile.

Our final recommendation for the main floor involved the back entry. It was a falsely labeled space that was neither a functional laundry nor a true back entry. We suggested that the laundry machines be moved to the basement so that the space could be reclaimed as a dedicated back entry with a good-sized closet and more open floor area. In this configuration, the entire family would be able to come to and from the garage at the same time much more effectively.

REVISING THE FORMAL LIVING ROOM AND BACK ENTRY

1 *Doorways to dining room closed off to create enclosed study space at front of house.*

2 *Built-in bookcases added to back of study wall for storage.*

3 *Coat closet added to provide storage, enclose front entry and separate it from the study.*

4 *Work desk placed in front of south facing window.*

5 *Laundry machines relocated to basement. Coat closet and bench added to improve functionality of back entry.*

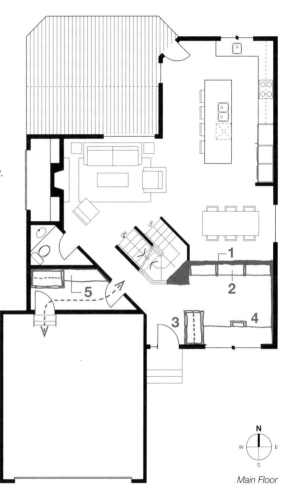

Main Floor

Looking at the sketch of the revised floor plan, Sarah looked relieved. "That's quite a change. It's hard to believe it's the same house. There seems to be so much more room."

"The main floor still isn't perfect," I said. "There's a privacy issue with the guest bathroom, and the rotated stair remains a problem. But at least their negative impact has been reduced because the living room furniture now faces away from the bathroom door, and the colliding geometry from the stair really only affects the side hallway."

"You mean our gallery," Tom joked. "So, what do we do on the second floor?"

Our recommendations for the second floor were much more modest, involving no significant change to the structure. In our experience, one of the biggest challenges anyone faces when fixing the design of a fast house is knowing when to stop. Tom and Sarah needed to be careful not to overspend. The interior of a house usually needs to be at least 20 years old for a major remodel to be a financially reasonable option. Their house was too new for any more substantive work to take place. Fortunately, the problems with the second floor bedrooms and bathrooms were not as high a priority for Tom and Sarah, particularly now that they would have a functional and pleasant library/office on the main floor.

"We have four simple suggestions," I said. "The first is to eliminate the falsely labeled 'study space' at the top of the stairs. Removing the built-in desk will make the circulation work much better."

Matthew told Tom and Sarah that our second suggestion was to stop pretending the library was anything more than a storage room. He drew a series of storage units along the back wall. Sarah liked that idea, since the lack of storage upstairs had been a big problem.

Our third suggestion was for the master bedroom. To create more closet storage, we relocated the bed into the middle of the room, facing the windows.

"Notice how this creates a space for a row of wardrobe units adjacent to the bathroom door," I said, as I drew over top of the plan. "The result is a nice dressing area with more than enough closet space."

REVISING THE UPPER FLOOR

1   Study desktop removed from upper stair landing to improve circulation.

2   Master bed located in center of room to improve connection with exterior view.

3   Free standing wardrobes create dressing area behind master bed and increase closet capacity.

4   Door swing reversed in master en-suite to avoid conflict with vanity.

5   Sink counter extended with additional under counter storage.

6   Free standing storage units added in former library.

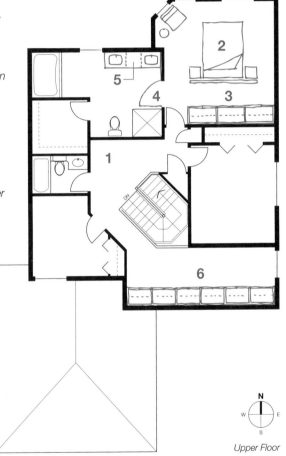

Upper Floor

"The room is now a more reasonable size, and it will be nice to have your bed closer to the windows," Matthew added.

Sarah gave these ideas the thumbs up. "They make our bedroom feel much nicer."

Finally, we suggested replacing the sink cabinet and counter in the en-suite. Extending it toward the window would give the couple extra counter space and drawer storage. We recommended that they save the existing cabinet and counter in case they decided to finish the basement bathroom.

"These are easy steps to take," Sarah said as we finished looking at the floor plans. "Based on these changes, I can see a future for us in this house."

"But what about the environmental problems with orientation and commuting?" Tom asked.

There wasn't much that could be done about the orientation of the house on the lot. That issue would be with this house forever. On the other hand, converting the formal living room into a study did make the situation slightly better. This south-facing room would now be used more often and Tom and Sarah will be able to take more advantage of the natural sunlight.

"The most important thing for you to remember is to not make the same mistake when you eventually go looking for your next home," I said.

"The same philosophy applies to location," Matthew added. "There's not much you can do right now, given the current situation, although it certainly helps that Tom is working from home at the moment. Just be sure and factor in the amount of driving you have to do when considering which house to buy next. It's a relatively easy way to make a dramatic reduction in your environmental footprint."

"And if the next owner of this house works in this part of the city, then he won't have that environmental problem either, right?" Tom said.

"That's the idea," I replied, as we stood up to leave.

TOM & SARAH'S COMPLETED REMODEL

Main Floor

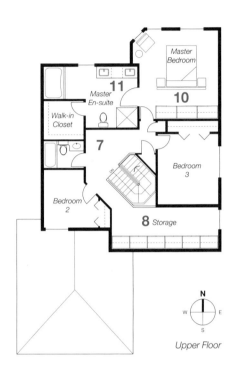

Upper Floor

Although it was not possible to address all of the problems with Tom and Sarah's house— such as the angled stair, the awkward guest bathroom location, and the poor solar orientation—many of the other design issues were able to be resolved in this remodel.

Colliding Geometries

1   Corner fireplace moved to side wall.
2   Angled kitchen counters and island replaced.

Redundant Spaces

3   Formal dining room becomes principal dining space.
4   Breakfast nook eliminated.
5   Formal living room becomes study space.

False Labeling

6   Foyer becomes enclosed front entry with closet.
7   Study loft desk removed.
8   Library becomes usable storage space.

Supersizing

9   Unnecessary kitchen appliances removed.
10 Wardrobe space added to master bedroom to make better use of floor area.
11 En-suite vanity enlarged to add more counter space and storage.

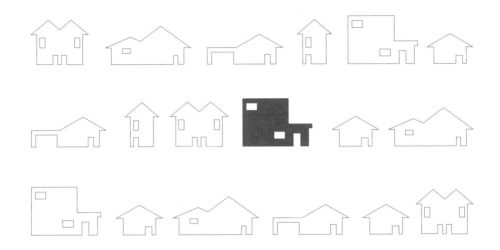

The Story of Luisa & Clara

SLOW FOOD — SLOW HOUSES

Fortunately, not all food and houses are fast.

The Slow Food Movement sprang to life in the mid-1980s as a response to fast food's assault on what and how we eat. Now a worldwide phenomenon, with local chapters throughout North America, Slow Food promotes a deeper and more intimate relationship between people and their food that is both healthy and environmentally sustainable. It supports local products, sustainable agricultural practices, and the pleasures of preparing and eating good food. In Carl Honoré's book *In Praise of Slow: How a Worldwide Movement is Challenging the Cult of Speed*, he explains, "Slow Food, as the name suggests, stands for everything that McDonalds does not; fresh local, seasonal produce, recipes handed down through generations; sustainable farming; artisanal production; and leisurely dining with family and friends." [9]

The Slow Food Movement's mandate is to oppose the standardization of taste, and to protect the cultural identities tied to our culinary traditions. "Slow Food helps people rediscover the joys of eating and understanding the importance of caring where their food comes from and how it's made." [10]

Slow Food offers a way of thinking about food that is based on its long-term value to our wellbeing, rather than the food industry's short-term economic gain. It focuses on locally sourced healthy ingredients that are carefully prepared and thoughtfully enjoyed. Slow Food offers a simple, effective way for each of us to re-engage with the food we eat. Slow Food is not a finished product you can buy, and the movement is not focused on expensive ingredients, extravagant preparations, or haute cuisine. It represents an attitude towards making smarter choices that are healthy for both you and the environment.

We can think about our houses in a similar way. A Slow Home stands for everything that a fast house does not: if a fast house is designed-to-be-sold, a Slow Home is designed to be lived in; if a fast house primarily benefits the balance sheet of the fast housing industry, a Slow Home is one that benefits the lives of the people who reside in it as well as the health of the planet.

9   Carl Honoré, *In Praise of Slow: How a Worldwide Movement is Challenging the Cult of Speed*, Toronto: Vintage, 2004, p. 59.

10   http://www.slowfood.com/international/1/about-us, Accessed Feb. 2011.

In the same way that Slow Food is carefully prepared, a Slow Home is thoughtfully designed. As Slow Food promotes local, naturally produced, healthy ingredients that reduce our environmental impact, a Slow Home is situated in a location that minimizes car use, is properly oriented to the sun, and incorporates environmental performance strategies. It responds to its climate, its site, and the real needs of the people who live in it. Finally, as Slow Food promotes the social dimension of enjoying a good meal, a Slow Home facilitates not just the functional needs of daily life but the broader social and emotional dimensions of home. When taken together, these features help make a Slow Home a more stable and profitable long-term investment for the homeowner than a fast house of equivalent size and cost.

Slow Food and Slow Homes are also part of a broader cultural trend towards a slower approach to life. Author Carl Honoré observes that increasingly, people are recognizing the frustrations and limitations of their over-stressed daily lives.

"The backlash against speed is moving into the mainstream with more urgency than ever before," Honoré writes. "Down at the grass roots, in kitchens, offices, concert halls, factories, gyms, bedrooms, neighborhoods, art galleries, hospitals, leisure centers, and schools near you, more and more people are refusing to accept the diktat that faster is always better. And in their many and diverse acts of deceleration lie the seeds of the global Slow movement." [11]

FOOD

Fast Food
Deceptive Ingredients:
> High Fat Content
> Excess Sugar
> Excess Salt

Supersized Portions
Limited Menu Choices

Slow Food
Locally Sourced Ingredients
Careful Preparation of Food
Culture of the Table

HOME

Fast House
Deceptive Design Features:
> Colliding Geometries
> False Labelling
> Redundant Spaces

Supersized Floor Areas
Limited Floorplan Options

Slow Home
Small Environmental Footprint
Thoughtfully Designed
High Livability

---

11   Honoré, p. 14.

In this context, fast and slow are more than just descriptors of a rate of change. According to Honoré, "They are shorthand for ways of being, or philosophies of life. Fast is busy, controlling, aggressive, hurried, analytical, stressed, superficial, impatient, active, quantity over quality. Slow is the opposite: calm, careful, receptive, still, intuitive, unhurried, patient, reflective, quality over quantity. It is about making real and meaningful connections – with people, culture, work, food, everything." [12] In these diverse ways, the people and ideas that comprise the Global Slow Movement are united by a simple goal – to live better in a fast-paced world.

Our homes are perhaps the most important place in which this kind of recalibration needs to occur. They are our most intimate spaces, the one place where we can retreat from the world, raise our children, and truly be ourselves. While it's ultimately the responsibility of each of us as individuals to build these kinds of deeper and more meaningful relationships with the world, a Slow Home can help in the process. In the same way that a sharp knife makes the preparation of a good meal easier and more enjoyable, a Slow Home can be an effective armature around which we can each start to create a richer, slower kind of life.

Unfortunately, like Tom and Sarah, many of us live in fast houses that make our daily routines more difficult, rather than better. Over time, we've become so accustomed to their shortcomings that, as we do when we cut tomatoes with the same old dull knife, we unconsciously compensate for their deficiencies, making the tool complete the task in spite of itself. It's not until we actually find a well-designed home (or a good sharp knife) that we realize how onerous and unacceptable the old situation really was. In the same way that we understand that sharpness is what makes a good knife effective, we need to understand the characteristics that define a Slow Home.

SIMPLE AND LIGHT

The challenge is that, on the surface at least, a Slow Home doesn't look that much different from a fast house. Slow Homes, like fast houses, run the gamut of size and type. They can be single-family houses, townhouses, or apartment/loft units in multi-family projects. Slow Homes can be new or old and they exist in all price ranges. Even a home's style, the types

---

12   Honoré, p. 15.

of finish used in it, and the details on its feature sheet don't reveal whether a house is fast or slow. That's because the distinguishing characteristics of a Slow Home are found in the fundamental design decisions that underlie the house. These basic design choices affect the nature of the individual rooms and how they fit together into a whole house, as well as how that house relates to the larger world around it.

The success or failure of every house depends on how consistently and thoughtfully these design decisions are made. A fast house fails because too many of these decisions are capricious and careless, made for expediency rather than livability. As we saw in Tom and Sarah's situation, these kinds of quantitative performance objectives only end up serving the fast housing industry and can seriously jeopardize the homeowner's quality of life.

The design decisions in a Slow Home, by contrast, are made according to a more qualitative set of guiding principles that put the long-term benefits to the homeowner and the environment at the forefront. The first of these guiding principles is that a Slow Home is simple to live in. The second is that it is also light on the environment.

SLOW HOME
GUIDING
PRINCIPLES

SIMPLE TO LIVE IN

FITS THE WAY YOU ACTUALLY LIVE

- Efficiently organized without wasted space

- Rooms are effectively sized and proportioned to fit their purpose

- Flexible long-term use

- Good natural daylight and ventilation

LIGHT ON THE ENVIRONMENT

REDUCES YOUR ENVIRONMENTAL FOOTPRINT

- Located close to work, school, and amenities to reduce car use

- Located in a walkable community

- Correctly oriented to sun and prevailing winds

- Conserves land, water and energy and makes a positive contribution to its community

A house that's simple to live in is one that's been designed to fit the way we actually live. In other words, it works properly. It maximizes livability and makes the routine tasks of daily life easier and more joyful to accomplish. Each of the rooms seamlessly accommodates its specific functions with no awkwardness or wasted space. This means that bedrooms are designed for sleeping and the storage of personal things, bathrooms are designed for the rituals that start and end each day, the kitchen is for cooking, the dining room for the enjoyment of a meal, and living areas are designed for all manner of social activities. At the same time, the house is also open and flexible so it can adapt to a wide variety of needs without requiring special, seldom-used spaces.

A house that's simple also feels good to be in. The rooms are the right size, they're well-proportioned, and they're easy to furnish for their purpose. They relate to each other in a logical fashion that eliminates any potential noise or privacy conflicts and results in a minimum amount of space devoted to hallways and circulation. The interior of the house is filled with natural light throughout the day and there's a strong connection to the outdoors, usually including an outdoor living area that extends the workings of the house out into nature.

But being simple to live in is only half of the story. A Slow Home also has to be light on the environment. From a design perspective, this can involve many different factors. At an interior level, it means making decisions like choosing rapidly renewable materials and low-impact finishes like VOC-free paint. From an exterior design point of view, it involves issues such as maximizing the thermal efficiency of the outside building envelope with high levels of insulation in the walls. At a technical level, it can mean specifying mechanical equipment that ensures the house consumes the least amount of nonrenewable energy and emits the least amount of greenhouse gases.

While design strategies such as these make critically important contributions to reducing the environmental footprint of a house, they are not, in and of themselves, sufficient. Sustainability is about more than just having all the latest technological devices. Being truly light on the environment also requires a more fundamental shift in the way we think about where and how we live. These changes in behavior and adjustments in attitude lay the groundwork for a more modest environmental footprint.

This means that before considering expensive mechanical systems like geo-thermal heating to reduce energy consumption, it's essential to ensure that the house is situated in a location that minimizes the amount of automobile commuting that's required each day. Before concentrating on low-flow toilets and LED lighting systems, it's important to ensure that the house is appropriately sized for the number of residents in order to avoid wasting energy to build and operate spaces that aren't often used. Before thinking about argon-filled triple pane windows, it's critical to confirm that the house is properly oriented to the sun and prevailing winds to facilitate natural heating and cooling in order to reduce the energy load on its mechanical systems. Finally, before considering the use of exotic finishing materials made from recycled content, it's important to ensure that the house is designed to be a worthy recipient of the land, materials and energy used in its construction, and that it effectively stewards those resources for the benefit of future generations.

These considerations of location, size, orientation, and stewardship don't replace the more detailed interior, exterior, and technical strategies, but they do form the foundation on which all these other environmental design initiatives need to rest. In the absence of a thoughtful design response to these more fundamental considerations of environmental responsibility, all of the other strategies lose their effectiveness and can too easily be converted into a green wash of marketing hype.

After all, an artisanal hand-rolled cigarette made with acid-free paper and fair trade organic tobacco is still likely to give you lung cancer. In the same way, a house that's fitted out with all the latest "environmental bling"—such as solar panels, low-flow toilets, and bamboo flooring—but continues to ignore the basics of location, size, orientation, and stewardship is still going to be bad for both you and the environment.

THE SLOW HOME TEST

"My name's Clara!" the young girl said to me as she extended her hand. "And this is my mom. Her name's Luisa."

Matthew and I had just finished answering questions after our public lecture and we were getting ready to leave the theater.

"Pardon us for bothering you, but we were wondering if you could give us some advice," Luisa said. "You see, we're looking to buy our first new home and after listening to your talk, we really want to find a Slow Home."

"It's going to be a two-bedroom loft!" Clara added enthusiastically.

"We've been looking at a lot of places over the last two months and we've narrowed our shortlist down to three properties. I'm just not sure which one we should pick, or if we should keep looking a little while longer," Luisa added.

As if on cue, Clara pulled a small envelope from her backpack. With a big smile, she handed it to Matthew. Her mom said, "If you have a minute, we brought the brochures with us and they all have floor plans."

We walked over to a table at the back of the room and sat down. After a brief conversation, we learned that Luisa was a single mother and that her daughter, who was 13, lived with her full-time. Luisa had just started a new job and with the increase in salary was now able to move out of the rental market and buy her first home. They were looking for a newly built and modestly sized two-bedroom apartment. Luisa and Clara were excited about the move but also serious about making the right choice.

"I understand the difference between a fast house and a Slow Home and I want my home to be simple to live in and light on the environment. I'm just not sure what to do next. Basically, I need to know how to find a Slow Home," Luisa said.

Matthew explained that we had distilled the Slow Home philosophy down to 12 design criteria that cover the most fundamental aspects of good residential design. Four of the criteria evaluate how light the house is on the environment. The remaining eight evaluate how simple it is to live in. We'd assigned points to each of the criteria according to their relative importance in the overall evaluation of design quality. All Luisa needed to do was work through each of the 12 criteria and add up the results.

"Interesting," said Luisa. "It sounds like a self-help test for your house."

"I have to admit that we did look at a few 'Cosmo quizzes' while working on it," Matthew joked.

"We call it the Slow Home Test," I said. "It's an effective way to determine whether the property you're looking at is a fast house, a Slow Home, or something in between."

Over the past 12 years, Matthew and I have completed countless property reviews for our clients, and we've seen firsthand the powerful difference that a design-centered property evaluation can make when buying a house. By reviewing its underlying design, we can quickly differentiate properties that would appear to be almost indistinguishable according to a conventional market comparison and a look at their feature sheets. With our design-focused evaluation augmenting the more traditional real estate information, our clients have been able to make more informed real estate decisions that ultimately result in the acquisition of a Slow Home and the pursuit of a simpler, lighter way of life.

The Slow Home Test evolved from the worksheet that Matthew and I used to keep notes during these property walkthroughs. When more and more clients began asking for a copy of the worksheet so that they could do their own evaluations, we added a basic scoring strategy and a short guide for understanding each of the criteria to create a simple do-it-yourself kind of test that anyone could use to evaluate the design quality of a home.

Pulling a blank Slow Home Test out of my briefcase, I said, "It's pretty easy to do. Once you've worked through the Test with us on these three properties, you should be able to use it on your own to evaluate the design of any other house."

Matthew explained that the Test has two parts, each worth a total of 10 points. The first part evaluates the 'house-in-the-world,' to determine how light the house is on the environment. The second part looks at the 'house-as-a-whole' and evaluates how simple the house is to live in.

"What do you mean by house-in-the-world?" Luisa asked.

"As you know, sustainability is about improving our relationship within the larger environment around us," I said. "So the design criteria in this section aren't as much about the design of the house itself as they are about the design of the house-in-the-world."

THE SLOW HOME TEST
Evaluate the Quality of the Design Underlying Any House

SLOW HOME STUDIO

The 12 Steps to a Slow Home			Yes	No
The House in the World	**1**	**Location** A Slow Home is located in a walkable neighborhood that is in proximity to work, shopping, and amenities in order to minimize the use of a car.	3	0
	2	**Size** A Slow Home is correctly sized to efficiently fit the needs of its residents in order to reduce unnecessary energy consumption and greenhouse gas emissions.	3	0
	3	**Orientation** A Slow Home is properly oriented to the sun, prevailing winds, and immediate surroundings in order to facilitate natural heating and cooling.	2	0
	4	**Stewardship** A Slow Home conserves land and water for future generations, reinforces smart, compact city growth patterns, and makes a positive contribution to the community.	2	0
The House as a Whole	**5**	**Entry** The front and back entries in a Slow Home are good-sized spaces of transition with adequate storage and, if possible, room for a bench.	1	0
	6	**Living** All indoor and outdoor living spaces in a Slow Home have good daylight, a natural focal point, and can accommodate a wide variety of uses without wasted space.	1	0
	7	**Dining** The dining area in a Slow Home is a day-lit space located close to the kitchen and can properly fit a table without any circulation conflicts.	1	0
	8	**Kitchen** The kitchen in a Slow Home is located outside of the main circulation route and has an efficient work triangle, continuous counter surfaces, and sufficient storage.	1	0
	9	**Bedrooms** All bedrooms in a Slow Home have good daylight, sufficient storage, a logical place for the bed, and enough room for circulation.	1	0
	10	**Bathrooms** All bathrooms in a Slow Home have private but accessible locations, are well-organized, modestly sized, and have sufficient counter space and storage.	1	0
	11	**Utility** A Slow Home has utility spaces for parking, laundry, mechanical equipment, and storage that are unobtrusively located, highly functional, and do not conflict with other uses.	1	0
	12	**Organization** A Slow Home is efficiently organized with like rooms grouped together and clear unobstructed circulation.	3	0

Minimum Design Quality Threshold *

0 - 6	7 - 12	13 - 16	17 - 20
Fast	Moderately Fast	Moderately Slow	Slow

/20

Score

The Slow Home Test evaluates how well a property conforms to the Slow Home Philosophy of being simple to live in and light on the environment. Plot your score on the bar graph and refer to the summary on the reverse page to interpret your results.
*** Properties that score below the Minimum Design Quality Threshold (13/20) don't sufficiently conform to the Slow Home philosophy and are not very simple or light places in which to live.*

Matthew elaborated. "Sustainability is a large and complex topic, and it's easy for people to get completely overwhelmed with information and not know what to do. The Slow Home Test simplifies all of this by focusing on the fundamental design issues that form the foundation on which all of the other sustainable strategies and products can be added. There's little point in getting all caught up in exotic choices like recycled countertops and geothermal heating if the environmental fundamentals of the house are wrong. It's like worrying about the recycled content of the deck chairs on the Titanic—interesting, but not especially useful when the ship is already starting to sink."

Matthew opened the envelope that Clara had given him and took out the three brochures.

"All of the apartments are about the same price," Luisa said, "and we liked each one for different reasons. Evergreen Estates has the biggest floor area. Bakerview Terrace has the nicest finishes and features, and Zoom Loft has a swimming pool."

From a quick review of the brochures, I learned that Evergreen Estates was a new low-rise development on the outskirts of town. The unit that Luisa and Clara liked was 1400 square feet and had three bedrooms, two and a half bathrooms, and a study. Bakerview Terrace was a new medium-rise development located in an established neighborhood close to downtown. The unit was 1200 square feet and had two bedrooms, two bathrooms, and a study. Zoom Loft was located in the same neighborhood. It was a medium-rise development that included the re-use of an old industrial building on the site. The unit that Luisa and Clara liked was in a new part of the project and was 1150 square feet with two bedrooms, two bathrooms, and a study.

LOCATION

Clara picked up the blank Slow Home Test and read our one-sentence evaluation for the first criteria. "A Slow Home is located in a walkable neighborhood that is in proximity to work, shopping, and amenities in order to minimize the use of a car."

"That makes sense," Luisa said, "but I'd never thought that commuting would be a design issue."

THE STORY OF LUISA & CLARA

Matthew explained that if we were going to think about the design of the house-in-the-world, we needed to consider how it would affect our overall environmental load. "The location of your home is a major determinant in how much driving you have to do," he said. "And because driving consumes so much energy and generates so many greenhouse gases, location is a big determinant of how light your house will be."

"So it's not an absolute value for a particular house, is it?" Luisa asked.

"Exactly," I answered. "It's about how well the location fits the rest of your life. All of the criteria in this first section evaluate the relationship of the house to either its residents or its surrounding context. The answers will vary for different families and different sites."

While looking at the Bakerview Terrace brochure, I discovered that there was a map on the back page showing the location of the project. I marked on the map the location of the other two properties that Luisa was considering and then asked her to add in her workplace, Clara's school, as well as any other places in the city that they regularly visited.

"The only other place I go to each week outside of regular grocery shopping and other chores is the dance studio," said Luisa. "I've been going there for years. It's my one bit of relaxation."

Looking at the annotated map, it was immediately clear that one of the projects, Evergreen Estates, was situated a considerable distance from the other parts of the city that they frequented. "It looks to me like you would have to do almost twice as much driving every day if you lived in Evergreen Estates," Matthew pointed out. "That's a big impact on your environmental footprint."

The next issue to evaluate was the walkability of the neighborhood. Walkability is a measure of how friendly a neighborhood is for pedestrians. Luisa informed us that both the Zoom Loft and Bakerview Terrace were located in an older neighborhood that had a nice shopping street within easy walking distance. Evergreen Estates, on the other hand, was in a new suburban community that only had a convenience store and gas station.

"It's a long walk," Clara said. "When we toured the apartment, I wanted to get a soda and it took me 15 minutes to walk to the store! Plus I had to go down a busy road that didn't even

EVALUATING LOCATION

15 Bakerview
Terrace

1024 sq ft Total*
2 Bedroom, 2 Full Bath + Den

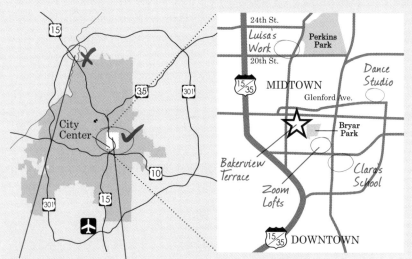

Evergreen Estates is on the edge of the city limits – 30 min. drive to downtown!

Bakerview Terrace and Zoom Lofts are both located in the City Center

Nearby Amenities

One Block From:
- Glenford Light Rail Station
- Cinema 21
- The Shops of Century Tower
- Urban Square Hotel

Two Blocks From:
- YMCA (City Center)
- Safeway & Econo-shop
- Restaurants on Glenford Ave
- Bryar Park Walking Trails and Bike Paths

City Life, Redefined.

have a sidewalk. In the end, I called my mom to come and pick me up for a ride back."

"Despite the name, we also didn't see any parks in Evergreen—just streets and houses," Luisa said.

Clara's experience confirmed my suspicion that the neighborhood suffered from low walkability. With a lack of continuous sidewalks, few public amenities, and almost no retail streets, Evergreen Estates was a neighborhood that had been designed for the car, not the pedestrian. As a result, it would be difficult for Luisa and Clara to reduce their automobile use when living there.

"The advantages extend beyond the environment," I said. "Studies have shown that residents of highly walkable neighborhoods weigh, on average, seven pounds less than those who live in car-dependent communities." [13]

"So we can lighten up in two ways with a good location," Luisa joked.

Matthew concluded, "Location's worth three points on the Slow Home Test. I think we should give the points to both Zoom Loft and Bakerview Terrace but not Evergreen Estates."

Luisa nodded in agreement.

SIZE

Clara read aloud the sentence for this criteria. "A Slow Home is correctly sized to efficiently fit the needs of its residents in order to reduce unnecessary energy consumption and greenhouse gas emissions."

"All three properties are about the same price, but with the Evergreen Estates unit, we get more space for the money," said Luisa. "Jorge, our real estate agent, told me that was a good thing. What do you think?"

---

13   Eric Pyrne, *2 Studies: Urban Sprawl Adds Pounds, Pollution*, The Seattle Times, January 26, 2006.

"It depends," replied Matthew. "The key issue here is to make sure that you aren't wasting energy and materials on unwanted or unnecessary spaces. The question is, do you need three bedrooms and bathrooms? If so, then the larger unit is a good idea. But my sense is that you would rarely use those extra rooms. The study could probably double up as a guest bedroom when necessary."

"You're right," Clara said. "My teacher said that if we all lived in smaller houses we could make our environmental footprints smaller."

"I understand that," Luisa said, with a frown. "But Jorge said that the biggest house is the best deal."

"That's the traditional way of looking at real estate," I said. "From a Slow Home point of view, you need to shift your thinking away from the quantity of space in the house and concentrate more on the quality of that space. In many situations, over-sizing a house is just a way to mask problems with the design. Instead of making the house work properly, the builder just adds another 100 square feet. It's kind of like compensating for a badly designed pair of jeans by purchasing the next size up. You may be able to do up the buttons but we all know that they still won't really fit you."

EVALUATING SIZE

Evergreen Estates 🌲	15 Bakerview Terrace	**ZOOM LOFTS**
1300 sq ft ✗	1055 sq ft ✓	1043 sq ft ✓
3 Bedroom Plus Den	*Third bedroom and half bath* 2 Bedroom Plus Study	2 Bedroom Plus Study
2.5 Bath	*not necessary for Luisa and Clara* 2 Bath	2 Bath

THE STORY OF LUISA & CLARA

"Or look all that good," Matthew said.

"So what about the other two?" asked Luisa.

Matthew replied, "They seem very reasonable. One thousand square feet is certainly not supersized for a two-bedroom apartment with a study. In fact, I think those apartments are good examples of modesty. As long as it's properly designed, a unit that size can be a great place to live."

"It says here that Size is worth three points on the Test," Clara said. "I'm going to give them to both Zoom Loft and Bakerview Terrace."

ORIENTATION

"A Slow Home is properly oriented to the sun, prevailing winds, and immediate surroundings in order to facilitate natural heating and cooling," Clara read from the Test.

"That sounds very technical. I don't know how to evaluate this one," Luisa admitted, looking concerned.

"Don't worry," I said. "It's pretty easy once you get the hang of it."

Understanding the impact of orientation on a house is not all that difficult. Up until the last 70 years of human history, almost everyone had at least a passing knowledge of how climate affected buildings because almost everyone depended on the sun and wind to at least partially heat and cool their homes. With the widespread introduction of central heating and air conditioning systems, that direct relationship between our personal comfort and the path of the sun or the direction of the wind was broken.

Today, one of the hallmarks of a fast house is a complete disregard for climate. It's a sealed box that relies on mechanical systems to regulate temperature. Unfortunately, these fossil-fueled systems consume a great deal of energy and generate a large amount of greenhouse gases, contributing in a major way to the environmental impact of our houses. Offloading at least some of these mechanical systems with natural means is an easy way for a house to be lighter on the environment.

"In a cold climate like the one we have here, it's possible to significantly reduce your environmental footprint by using the sun's energy to help heat and light your home," Matthew explained.

"Does that mean that the apartment needs a solar panel?" asked Clara.

"No," I said. "This way of using solar energy doesn't require any fancy equipment. You just need to make sure the house faces the right way. When evaluating the orientation of a house, the first thing to remember is that sunlight comes from the east in the mornings, south during the day and west in the late afternoon and evenings. During the winter in a cold climate region, the goal is usually to get as much sunlight into the house as possible. In the summer, the situation changes a bit because the light coming from the west in the late afternoon can cause significant overheating. That's because the summer sun is low on the horizon at that time of day, and the rays can extend deep into the interior. While that's very advantageous in the winter, it's something to avoid in the summer whenever possible."

In the summer, the wind can be used to naturally keep things cool. All that's really required for good cross-ventilation are windows in one part of the house to let the breezes in, and other windows, preferably located some distance away, that let the breezes out. Both the Bakerview Terrace and Zoom loft were corner units. With windows on two sides, they should have more than enough cross ventilation to keep the interiors cool in the summer. The Evergreen Terrace unit, although not in a corner location, also had a significant amount of exterior window surface and should have sufficient cross ventilation.

To evaluate their solar orientation, Matthew had drawn a sun path diagram on each of the floor plans. Looking at the drawings, it immediately became clear that two of the units were not well-oriented to the sun.

"The unit in Evergreen Estates faces north," I observed, "so it will never have any direct sunlight. This means the interior won't benefit from the natural heat of the sun, and you'll need to use electric lights more often. Both of these are bad for your environmental footprint."

EVALUATING ORIENTATION

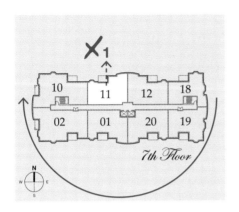

This unit does not have good solar orientation for the cold climate in which it is located. All of the windows face north (1). As a result, the interior will get very little direct sunlight.

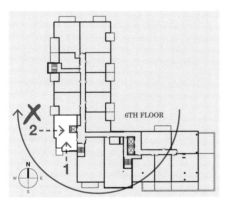

15 Bakerview Terrace

This unit has a mixed solar orientation. The south facing windows (1) will let sufficient sunlight into the unit during the day; however, the west facing windows (2) will create unwanted afternoon heat gain in the summer months.

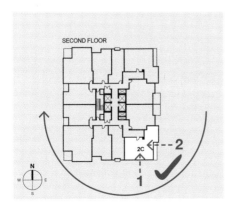

ZOOM LOFTS

This unit has a good solar orientation. The south facing (1) and east facing (2) windows will let sufficient sunlight into the unit in the morning and early afternoon while avoiding heat gain from the west summer sun.

`The Bakerview Terrace apartment was also a problem. It predominantly faced west, which meant that the major living space and the master bedroom would be overheated by the sun in the afternoon.

"But the Zoom Loft is good, right?" asked Luisa. "It faces south and that means it gets sunlight throughout the day."

"Correct," said Matthew. "And the other side faces east, so it will get morning sun. You won't have to worry about overheating in the afternoon."

"Orientation is worth two points on the Slow Home Test," I said to Clara.

"Then there's two more points for Zoom!" she responded with a smile.

STEWARDSHIP

"What does stewardship mean?" Clara asked.

Strictly speaking, the word means to watch over and take care of something that belongs to somebody else. We use it in the Slow Home philosophy to describe the idea that designing a house shouldn't be a selfish activity that's only concerned with the wellbeing of its residents. The design also needs to take care of the natural environment by conserving land and water for future generations. In addition, it needs to take care of the community by making a positive contribution to the neighborhood in which it's located.

"Let me give you an example of what I mean," I said. "If someone cut down a mature tree to make toothpicks, you would be upset, right? I think that we would all agree that turning a majestic tree into a mass-produced throw-away product is a waste. But what if, instead of toothpicks, the tree was used to create a series of handmade rocking chairs? Because of their comfort and sturdy construction, people liked to use them to rock babies to sleep, spend time with friends, and quietly read. Over time, they became treasured family heirlooms that were lovingly looked after and passed down from one generation to the next.

I would argue that the chairs were a fair trade for the tree. In this case, unlike the toothpick scenario, cutting down the tree was not an environmental degradation, because the chairs were worthy recipients of the materials and energy that originally made up the tree. Plus the long life of the rocking chairs meant that the owners actually conserved resources by not having to buy a bunch of other, less well-made, chairs. Finally, as heirlooms passed down from one generation to the next, the chairs help sustain the family's history.

We need to start thinking about our houses in the same kind of way. They should be well-designed, high quality places to live in order to be worthy of all the materials and energy that go into their creation. Stewardship means that we need to take a responsible approach to the future when making decisions about our houses today.

"But what does stewardship mean when we look at these three properties?" Luisa asked.

Matthew read the criteria for stewardship. "A Slow Home conserves land and water for future generations, reinforces smart, compact city growth patterns, and makes a positive contribution to the community."

Because Luisa and Clara were looking for a higher density apartment style of house, all of the properties used land much more efficiently than a single family house. Higher density development also increases the efficiency of city utilities and infrastructure.

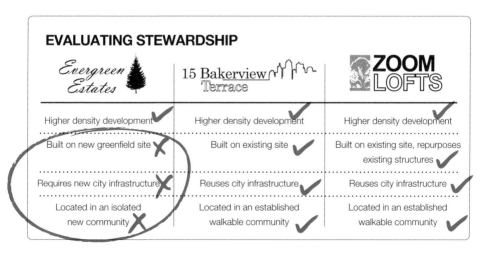

Once again, however, I had a concern with Evergreen Estates. The development was located on the edge of the city in a new master-planned community that, two years before, had been productive farmland. This kind of so-called "Greenfield" development is not as environmentally responsible as the other two projects, which were built on existing "Brownfield" sites in established communities. Evergreen Estates contributes to a sprawling city form that requires the construction of new roads, utilities, and other amenities, promotes ever more automobile use, and draws tax money from developing areas of denser public use. None of this is light on the environment.

Bakerview Terrace, on the other hand, conserves energy by reusing not only the site on which it's located, but also all of the city roads and services that have existed in the community for over 50 years. The repurposing of the embodied energy that already exists in these systems is an effective way to lighten our environmental load. The Zoom Loft took the idea of reuse one step further, as the project also included the repurposing of two abandoned industrial buildings on the site.

Finally, by reinvesting in existing neighborhoods, both projects bring new life to an older community.

"I see from the Test that Stewardship is worth two points," Luisa remarked. "Based on what you've said, I'm going to give them to both the Zoom Loft and Bakerview Terrace."

With the first part of the Test complete, I suggested that Clara add up the results.

"Evergreen Estates didn't get any points!" Clara said, with a barely disguised sense of glee. "I haven't liked that place since my long walk to the gas station."

Bakerview Terrace scored much better with 8/10 points and the Zoom Loft had a perfect score of 10/10. At this stage, at least, it looked as though both were well on their way to being Slow Homes. Even if the unit in Evergreen Estates had a perfect score in the next house-as-a-whole section, however, it still wouldn't have a score that was sufficient to be considered a Slow Home.

"I think he's trying to tell us that we need to ditch it," Clara told her mother.

"I'm completely okay with that," Luisa said, sighing. "I'd come to the same conclusion myself after listening to the analysis. But, I have to say, when we sat down with you today, that property was my front-runner. I guess I got taken in by its size."

"It happens all too often," Matthew said.

Setting the Evergreen Estates feature sheet aside, I suggested that it was time to move on to the second half of the Test and evaluate the design quality of the house-as-a-whole for these two properties.

"Basically, we're going to evaluate each of the major rooms and then look at how well they all fit together in the overall organization of the house," I said.

"So now we get to the fun part," said Clara, grinning. "I love the way you guys pointed out all of the problems with those fast houses in the lecture."

"Let's hope there isn't too much fun right now," Luisa said. "I'm still hoping that at least one of these apartments is a Slow Home."

LUISA & CLARA'S FLOORPLAN OPTIONS

ENTRY

Clara began by reading the sentence for the next criteria in the Test. "The front and back entries in a Slow Home are good-sized spaces of transition with adequate storage and, if possible, room for a bench."

"The important thing to remember is that an entry is a space and not just a door," Matthew said. "The door is there for security and to keep the weather out, but you also need a defined space once you get inside that is at least somewhat separate from the rest of the house."

Reviewing the plans, it was clear that the front entry in the Zoom Loft was well-designed. The minimum dimension was about 5', which is an appropriate size to allow two or three people to use the space at the same time. There was a good-sized closet conveniently located near the door, and even enough room for Luisa to add a small bench.

"I like that idea," Luisa said as I hand-drew it onto the plan. "It would be great to be able to sit down when I put on my winter boots."

"The other positive thing about this entry is how it relates to the rest of the house," I said. "Notice how you don't have to pass through the entry to get to any other space. That's a good feature when the floor is wet from rain and snow or Clara and her friends just drop all their school backpacks and lunch bags at the door."

Unfortunately, the Bakerview Terrace apartment didn't have a successful entry. With a minimum dimension of 3', it was really more of a hallway than a space. There was only enough room for one person to use the space at a time, and everyone else would have to line up outside the door or down the hall. Although the closet was a generous size, it was located too far away from the entry to be convenient. The result was an additional walk down the hall and around the corner every time a forgotten coat or scarf needed to be retrieved. Finally, the space didn't relate well to the rest of the apartment, as the doors to both the family bathroom and kitchen opened directly into the entry. Anything left on the floor of this small space and there would almost certainly be something on the floor, given the distance to the closet — would obstruct access to these two well-used rooms.

"All of the criteria for the individual rooms on the Slow Home Test are worth one point," Matthew said.

"Okay," said Luisa. "I think Zoom Loft gets the point for entry, and Bakerview Terrace doesn't."

Clara, Matthew and I all nodded in agreement.

LIVING

This time it was Matthew who read the criteria aloud. "All indoor and outdoor living spaces in a Slow Home have good daylight, a natural focal point, and can accommodate a wide variety of uses without wasted space."

Good daylight is obviously critical for any space in which you intend to spend a significant amount of time. In an apartment/loft type house this can be difficult to achieve when the units are narrow and deep. The two homes Luisa had shortlisted were corner units, however, and, given their solar orientations, we knew that they would both have ample light. The one exception to this positive evaluation was the study space in Bakerview Terrace. It was a windowless room in the middle of the floor plan.

"This is an example of a falsely labeled space," I said, pointing to the oversized closet that had been labeled as a study. "Nobody's going to want to spend much time in there."

"He's right," Clara said. "I'd choose the study in Zoom Loft any day. Just look at the size of that window. And it's close to my room, so I can keep my computer in there."

Luisa smiled as Matthew turned our attention to the living room.

"To evaluate the design quality of the main living spaces, we need to understand how well they can be furnished," Matthew said, as he sketched a furniture layout into both floor plans. It quickly became obvious that one of the living spaces worked much better than the other. In the Zoom Loft, the solid wall between the two south-facing windows offered a natural place for the TV, creating a focal point around which the rest of the furniture could be organized.

Matthew centered a three-piece sofa on the TV and placed a chair on the left to create a comfortable seating area while still allowing enough space to easily circulate to the terrace.

COMPARING PLANS - ENTRY AND LIVING

1 The front entry is adequately sized with a coat closet in close proximity and room for a bench.

2 The living area has lots of natural light and a direct connection with the outside terrace. The short wall between the windows is a natural location for the TV.

3 The outdoor deck is too narrow to be furnished properly.

4 The study is properly sized and has good natural light.

"Look at how well it all fits," Clara said excitedly.

The same could not be said for the Bakerview apartment. The size and proportion of the space were not good and, as a result, the layout was cramped.

"Notice how the only real place for the sofa is against the short side wall," Matthew said, "and we have to put a chair in the opposite corner so as not to obstruct the door to the terrace. After doing that there isn't really enough space for a coffee table and no natural place for the TV. All of this is going to make the living space feel small and cramped."

"I don't like that very much," Clara said.

I suggested that we finish off by looking at the outdoor terraces. They needed to be considered, just like any other living space.

15 Bakerview Terrace

1   The front entry is too narrow to be effective and does not have a closet.

2   The living area has lots of natural light but it is too small to properly fit a furniture grouping and there is no logical place for a tv.

3   The outdoor terrace is a good size and proportion and can be easily furnished as a living space.

4   The study is a falsely labeled space. It is an interior room with no natural light or ventilation.

Clara said, "I think the Zoom Loft balcony is too narrow for furniture. It would be a great place for hopscotch, though."

"You have a good eye," I said. "You're right. The outdoor space in Bakerview Terrace is a much better size and shape for furniture."

"That's okay," said Luisa. "I think we should still give the Zoom Loft the point for living even though the terrace isn't great. The study and living room are good and the truth is, I don't think we're going to spend all that much time on the balcony. I'm a little scared of heights."

"But no points for Bakerview," Clara added.

DINING

"A dining table is important to us," Luisa said. "We have breakfast together every morning and we try to have a home-cooked dinner as a family at least four times a week."

"That's impressive and also rather slow – in a good way," Matthew said as he began to read the sentence for the next criteria. "The dining area in a Slow Home is a day-lit space located close to the kitchen and can properly fit a table without any circulation conflicts."

Picking up the Zoom Loft floor plan, I drew in a round four-person dining table centered on the blank wall to the left side of the space. "This dining space has real potential. Luisa, if you buy this unit, I suggest hanging a large painting or other framed image in the middle of this side wall. It will create a visual focus that will anchor the table in the room. If you had a closed-in formal dining room there would be an obvious place for the table in the center of the room, but in an open plan space, you need to use a focal point like this to visually organize the furniture."

The Zoom Loft dining area was well-designed. The space was appropriately sized and well-proportioned. There was enough room to easily move around the table and there were no conflicts with any of the main circulation routes in the house. Like the living room and kitchen, this part of the house would also get plenty of light throughout the day and be a pleasant place in which to sit.

I noted that the kitchen island had been extended an extra foot in width to create an informal eating space with room for two or three stools located outside of the main circulation route. The result was a convenient area for a casual meal, as well as a nice place for guests to sit while Luisa was working in the kitchen.

Switching our attention to Bakerview Terrace, I knew from the previous section that there were going to be problems with dining. The open plan space was just too small and badly proportioned to accommodate both a seating area and a table. Like so many combined living/dining rooms, it was a falsely labeled space. The reality was that there wasn't really enough room for a table. I squeezed one into the drawing anyway so as to show Luisa and Clara how many awkward problems it created for both living and dining.

"Why would they make a house without a dining room? Where are you supposed to eat?" Clara asked, frowning.

That was a good question. Falsely labeled spaces like this are usually the result of a careless design process where no one has taken the time to consider how the rooms would actually be furnished for use. In the end, they are nothing more than labels on a plan, intended to make a poorly designed house look better than it really is.

The eating bar was little better. "Notice how the stools are too close to the dining table. This is going to make them awkward for someone to use. I'm afraid this is not a good place for anyone to sit," Matthew concluded.

Shaking her head, Clara recorded one point for the Zoom Loft.

KITCHEN

It was Luisa's turn to read the sentence for the next criteria. "The kitchen in a Slow Home is located outside of the main circulation route and has an efficient work triangle, continuous counter surfaces, and sufficient storage."

"My mom wants a nice kitchen. She likes to cook," Clara announced proudly.

Picking up the Zoom Loft plan, Matthew quickly drew a triangle between the three major appliances. "This kitchen has a good work triangle. It's an effective size and shape. Oversized work triangles just add too many steps for the cook."

"Notice how the work triangle is located at one end of the kitchen," I added. "That creates a two- zone layout with one area for cooking and another for preparation. That way you can be working in one zone while Clara's in the other."

The Zoom Loft also met Luisa's expectations for cooking in other ways. It had plenty of storage and there were large areas of continuous counter surface to work on. The kitchen window was a bonus. Although the open plan configuration meant that the kitchen

COMPARING PLANS - DINING AND KITCHEN

1   The dining area is properly sized to accommodate a table. The side wall is a natural focal point on which to center the table while still leaving room for circulation.

2   The kitchen is a light filled space that is well connected to the principal living areas. The appliance triangle is efficient and there is sufficient counter space and storage.

3   The eating bar is conveniently organized and well sized.

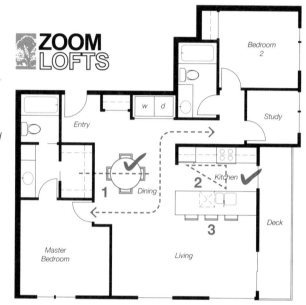

would have lots of natural light throughout the day, the window would provide a more immediate view of the outside in addition to some much-needed natural ventilation.

Turning to the Bakerview Terrace floor plan, I saw that the poor design thinking we had seen so far in our evaluation continued into this part of the unit. The kitchen had a much larger floor area than the one in the Zoom Loft but it was not functional. In fact, it had less counter space and storage than the other kitchen.

"If you like to cook, you're not going to like this kitchen," I concluded. "There isn't much work surface for food preparation, and there aren't many cabinets."

"That's interesting," Luisa said. "I don't remember this kitchen having a bad layout when we did our tour. But now, when I look at the plan, it seems silly."

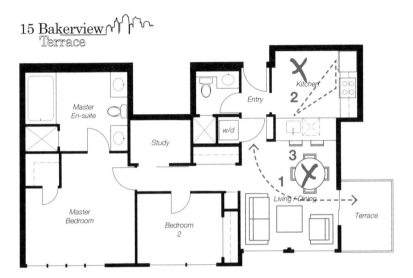

15 Bakerview Terrace

1   The combined living/dining room is a falsely labeled space. There is insufficient floor area for a table without creating a conflict with the eating bar and obstructing access to both the living room and the outdoor terrace.

2   The kitchen does not have sufficient daylight. There is wasted floor area and the appliance triangle is awkward.

3   The eating bar stools conflict with the dining table.

"That's a common problem," I told Luisa. "And it's one that many people don't recognize until they start using the kitchen. On first glance, this would look like a big kitchen, but it's really just inefficient. No one is going to use that space in the corner for anything, except maybe to store the recycling."

"They really should have made the floor area of the kitchen smaller and reallocated the space to make a bigger area for the dining table," Matthew said, shaking his head.

I drew in the work triangle for this kitchen. "Here's another problem. The refrigerator and the cook-top are too close together and the sink is too far away. I'm also worried because the work triangle is so long and narrow. This indicates that it will be difficult for more than one person to use the kitchen at the same time."

Finally, the kitchen suffered from a lack of light. "It's kind of shoved into the corner of the unit and located quite a distance from the windows. I think it's going to be a little dim in there," Matthew concluded.

"I've seen enough," Luisa said. "Clara, give one point for the kitchen in Zoom Loft and nothing for Bakerview Terrace."

BEDROOMS

This time, I took a turn reading out the criteria. "All bedrooms in a Slow Home have good daylight, sufficient storage, a logical place for the bed, and enough room for circulation."

From our review of orientation, I knew that the bedrooms in both units had properly sized windows that provided a good amount of sunlight. I took a few minutes to sketch the bed and dressers onto the plan.

"The first step to evaluating the design quality of a bedroom is to draw in the furniture," I remarked. "Over the years, we have seen too many spaces that are either too small or awkwardly shaped to properly fit a bed."

Luisa said she would have found that hard to believe before going through the Slow Home Test, but she certainly believed it now. As we'd expected, given the many positive features of the Zoom Loft that we'd already discovered, its bedrooms were well-designed. Both were properly sized and proportioned so that the bed would fit comfortably, with sufficient space to move around the room. The closets were also well-sized and conveniently located.

"Notice how the bed in the master bedroom is centered on the facing wall," Matthew said. "That makes visual sense and will work well if you want to have a TV. Placing the bed in that location moves it closer to the window and also creates more space at the other end of the room for the circulation zone between the bedroom door and the closet."

"Very clever," Luisa said, nodding. "I like this room."

The bedrooms in the Bakerview Terrace unit were more problematic. Although the master bedroom was significantly larger than it was in the Zoom Loft, its shape made the space much less functional.

"Look at all that wasted space by the door," Matthew said. "What exactly are you supposed to do in there except walk to the bathroom? Plus there's too much space at the end of the bed. The TV will be too far away."

Even more frustrating was the fact that despite all of that extra space, the area around the bed was tight. In fact, it was barely wide enough to accommodate a bed and two side tables. This was unacceptable for a room with that amount of floor area.

My last concern in the master bedroom was with the closet. Although it was a well-sized walk-in, the door was located so that it opened directly onto the bed. "That's just sloppy design," I said in a frustrated tone. "There's no reason that the door couldn't have been located on the other wall, beside the bathroom. It would be more convenient in the morning and you wouldn't have to look inside your closet every night."

Moving on to the second bedroom, Clara immediately noticed that I had drawn the bed in the corner of the room right up against the window. "Why did you do that? It's hard enough for me to make my bed as it is. How can I do it when the bed is shoved into the corner?"

"Look at the door swing," Matthew suggested. "Putting it in the corner is the only way to avoid having the door hit the end of the bed. This is an unfortunate room."

Clara added one more point for the Zoom Loft and none for Bakerview Terrace.

BATHROOMS

"I'm going to get my own bathroom!" Clara said excitedly.

"Lucky you," Matthew replied. "Let's see which one's best."

COMPARING PLANS - BEDROOMS BATHROOMS AND UTILITY SPACES

1   The second bedroom is well sized to fit a bed. It has an effective closet and good natural light.

2   The main bathroom is a standard layout in a private but accessible location that is also convenient for guests.

3   The master bedroom and en-suite are appropriately sized and effectively organized.

4   The laundry is in a convenient location with adequate space in front of the machines.

Luisa read out the criteria. "It says here that all bathrooms in a Slow Home have private but accessible locations, are well-organized, modestly sized and have sufficient counter space and storage."

The second bathroom that Clara would be using would also have to do double duty as the designated guest bathroom in both houses. Although this is fairly typical in two-bedroom units of that size, it does mean that extra attention needs to be paid to the bathroom's location, in order to ensure that it works well for both types of users.

In the Bakerview Terrace apartment, the second bathroom was located by the front door. While this was handy for guests, it would be much less convenient for Clara's everyday use. The proximity to the entry also meant that she would always be walking through the boots and shoes at the front door every time she went to the bathroom.

15 Bakerview Terrace

1   The second bedroom is too narrow and the door swing conflicts with the bed.

2   The main bathroom is small, has no storage and is located too far away from bedroom 2.

3   The master bedroom is oversized and the closet is insufficient.

4   The en-suite has wasted floor space, an awkward toilet location and insufficient counter space and storage.

5   The access to the laundry is awkward because it is located in a narrow hallway.

Inside the bathroom, the situation was little better. The space was small and there was no room in the sink cabinet for drawers. The situation did not look happy for a teenaged girl.

In the Zoom Loft, on the other hand, the second bathroom was a more standard layout. The cabinet was extended to provide a bank of drawers to the right of the sink. Although still modest in size, the room would be more than adequate for Clara's needs. The location of the bathroom in the plan was also good. It was not too far away from the main living spaces for guests, and, with the door right outside Clara's room, it would be convenient for her.

"That sounds great," Clara said. "I like the idea of having all those drawers. Mom and I share a bathroom right now and it's overflowing with stuff."

"What about my bathroom?" Luisa asked softly.

The en-suite in the Bakerview apartment was clearly supersized. In fact, it was bigger than Clara's bedroom. Despite all the floor area, however, it wasn't particularly functional. The two sink cabinets were small and didn't have any storage. The placement of the toilet in between the two sinks was awkward, if not slightly bizarre, and there was a huge amount of floor space in the middle of the room.

"That would be great if you want to do hot yoga in your bathroom," Matthew said, laughing. "But it might get a bit slippery!"

Shifting our attention to the Zoom Loft plan, it was clear that here, too, the design was much superior. The master bathroom was more reasonably sized and, although it didn't have a separate shower, there was lots of counter space and drawers as well as a full-height storage cabinet on the right end of the vanity.

"The best part of this layout is that the closet opens into the sink area and the toilet and bathtub are in their own space. That will be convenient when you're getting ready in the morning," Matthew said. "And with this layout, the high humidity from the bathtub won't affect you when you're putting on your makeup."

Clara marked down one more point for the Zoom Loft on the Slow Home Test.

UTILITY

Clara enthusiastically noted that there were only two questions left on the Test as Matthew began to read the next criteria. "A Slow Home has utility spaces for parking, laundry, mechanical equipment, and storage that are unobtrusively located, highly functional, and do not conflict with other uses."

The evaluation of the utility spaces for these two homes only needed to consider the laundry areas. Both units had a single underground parking space and a well sized storage locker in the basement. They were almost identical in each project and more than adequate.

As would be expected in an apartment-style unit of this size, the washer and dryer in both homes were located in a closet rather than in a dedicated laundry room. While there is certainly nothing wrong with this configuration, it does mean that particular attention needs to be paid to the location of the closet within the overall floor plan, as well as ensuring that there is an appropriate amount of space in front of the doors.

Referring everyone's attention to the Zoom Loft floor plan, I noted that this house had a good laundry. It was located in the open circulation area between the entry and the hallway to Clara's bedroom, so it was accessible but still somewhat removed from the action. There was also plenty of floor area in front of the doors so when Clara and Luisa were doing laundry, the basket wouldn't be in the way.

"That sounds great," Luisa said. "Clara promised me that she was going to start doing her own laundry when we moved into our new house. With all her clothes, we're going to need all the laundry space we can get."

Clara didn't look all that amused.

The laundry situation in Bakerview Terrace was not as successful. The stacked washer/dryer unit was located in a closet beside the second bathroom. The doors opened into the narrow hallway that connected the entry, kitchen and bathroom to the rest of the apartment.

"Look at that location," Matthew exclaimed. "It's got to be the worst!"

Luisa looked a little confused, so Matthew elaborated. "When you're doing the laundry, you need room to spread out. Too often a laundry closet seems to be designed just to store the machines but not really use them. When I do laundry, the basket and sometimes even a pile of clothes end up sitting in front of the machines. In this unit, they would be sitting right in the middle of that little hallway. What happens when the doorbell rings or you have to go to the bathroom or the kitchen? It'll be a tripping nightmare!"

"It's also a little public," I added. "That closet is quite open to the main living space."

Luisa smiled. "Okay! You've convinced me. I'll never think about laundry the same way again."

COMPARING PLANS - ORGANIZATION

1   The hallway to the study,
    main bathroom, and
    bedroom 2 is minimized
    and efficient.

2   The split bedroom plan
    increases privacy.

3   The principal spaces are
    appropriately scaled for
    the size of the unit.

4   The circulation through
    the dining and living
    areas is clear and
    unobstructed.

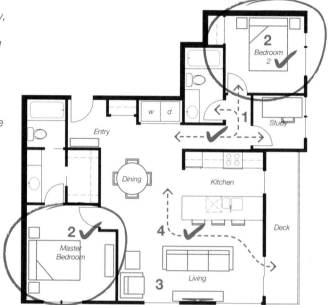

"You all spend too much time thinking about washing clothes," Clara said, shaking her head.

"But it's one more point for Zoom Loft anyway," Luisa said.

ORGANIZATION

"Last criteria," I said, "but it's an important one. Organization is worth three points on the Slow Home Test."

So far we'd been looking at the design quality of each individual room, Matthew pointed out. Now we needed to look at how well all those spaces fit together to create the whole home.

15 Bakerview Terrace

1   *The hallway to the bedrooms is too long and narrow.*

2   *The master bedroom is disproportionately large while the second bedroom is too small.*

3   *The master en-suite is disproportionately large for the size of the unit.*

4   *The circulation in the living/dining area is obstructed by the furniture.*

"How do we do that?" Clara asked. "It says here that a Slow Home is efficiently organized with like rooms grouped together and clear unobstructed circulation."

"It's actually not all that complicated," I said. "We want to see if the spaces are organized together in a logical way or if they're just a haphazard collection of rooms. Generally, I look for a clustering of uses so there's a clear distinction between the private bedroom areas and the more public areas. This helps to avoid any privacy or acoustic conflicts. I also want to make sure that the proportion of space devoted to each room makes sense. There's little point in having a huge kitchen at the expense of bedroom size. Finally, I look to see if there are wasted areas in the plan, which are either too small or too awkwardly shaped to be useful. This includes overly long hallways."

After having spent the past 20 minutes examining the Zoom Loft plan for all of the previous design criteria, I'd already come to the conclusion that the unit was very well organized. First of all, as a corner unit, there was no problem with natural light or ventilation in any of the rooms. Second, the hallway was short and effective with a clear circulation route through the main open-plan living area that easily allowed movement without conflicting with the furniture. Third, all of the rooms were not only well-sized for their own purposes but also appropriately proportioned in relation to each other, so that everything was in balance. Finally, there seemed to be no wasted space in the plan.

"I think the split bedroom configuration would be ideal for you two," Matthew said. "Even in a relatively small apartment, it will give you both some much-needed privacy. "

"I see what you mean," Luisa said. "Clara likes to listen to music and I like to go to bed early. In our current apartment, our rooms are side-by-side and it can get a little tense sometimes."

"This way, you only have to worry about Clara's music bothering the neighbors," Matthew said, with a grin.

Turning our attention to the Bakerview Terrace plan, I noted that it was also a corner unit and that all of the spaces had good daylight and natural ventilation. In terms of circulation, I reminded Luisa and Clara about the conflicts at the entry as well as the potential for problems when moving through the main living area. But it was the way that the spaces were proportioned in relationship to each other that was my major concern with the organization of this apartment.

"Overall, this unit is a bit bigger than the Zoom Loft, but it doesn't feel like it," I told Luisa. "In the end, there's not enough room allocated to the main living areas. As we saw when we did the furniture layouts, the living, dining and kitchen areas are just too cramped."

"It's the supersized master bathroom and bedroom that throw off the balance," Matthew added. "They make no sense."

Luisa nodded as Clara completed the Slow Home Test by awarding the final three points for organization to the Zoom Loft. The Bakerview Terrace apartment did not receive the points.

ADDING IT UP

As Clara tallied up the Test results for the two properties, I already knew that we had a clear winner. The Zoom Loft was a well-designed house. In fact, it was a great example of a Slow Home, embodying the principles of being simple to live in and light on the environment.

"20/20! That's cool!" exclaimed Clara.

"Having a perfect score is exceptional," said Matthew. "And, best of all, this Slow Home doesn't cost any more than the other two properties on your shortlist that were nowhere near as well-designed."

This was certainly true. The Bakerview Terrace apartment only had a score of 8/20. I told Luisa and Clara that any new house with a score that low is not one that we would recommend buying.

Luisa had a big grin on her face. "That's really interesting. Until we went through this process, I have to admit all three of these properties looked very much the same to me. As I said earlier, I probably would've just picked the one that had the most amount of space for the least amount of money."

"That's what most people do," I said. "And the result is that, more often than not, they end up living in a poorly designed fast house."

"I think the problem is that most people don't know much about design quality," said Matthew. "As a result, they base their home-buying decision on more superficial issues."

"You mean it's like picking a cell phone because you like the color of the case?" Clara asked, smiling.

Luisa jumped in. "Well, we aren't going to do that this time, sweetheart. We're making the smart choice now."

Armed with this information, Luisa told us that she intended to contact her realtor and begin to negotiate the purchase of the Zoom Loft.

We advised her that although an understanding of design quality should be a critical factor in every real estate decision, it's not the only issue to consider. The more traditional metrics of price, comparable values, financing, legal conditions, and the overall condition of the interior remain valid and extremely important.

The Slow Home approach to buying a home does not negate these issues, but augments them with an informed analysis of design quality.

THE SLOW HOME TEST
Evaluate the Quality of the Design Underlying Any House

The 12 Steps to a Slow Home			Evergreen	Bakerview	Zoom
The House in the World	**1 Location** A Slow Home is located in a walkable neighborhood that is in proximity to work, shopping, and amenities in order to minimize the use of a car.		0	3	3
	2 Size A Slow Home is correctly sized to efficiently fit the needs of its residents in order to reduce unnecessary energy consumption and greenhouse gas emissions.		0	3	3
	3 Orientation A Slow Home is properly oriented to the sun, prevailing winds, and immediate surroundings in order to facilitate natural heating and cooling.		0	0	2
	4 Stewardship A Slow Home conserves land and water for future generations, reinforces smart, compact city growth patterns, and makes a positive contribution to the community.		0	2	2
The House as a Whole	**5 Entry** The front and back entries in a Slow Home are good-sized spaces of transition with adequate storage and, if possible, room for a bench.		–	0	1
	6 Living All indoor and outdoor living spaces in a Slow Home have good daylight, a natural focal point, and can accommodate a wide variety of uses without wasted space.		–	0	1
	7 Dining The dining area in a Slow Home is a day-lit space located close to the kitchen and can properly fit a table without any circulation conflicts.		–	0	1
	8 Kitchen The kitchen in a Slow Home is located outside of the main circulation route and has an efficient work triangle, continuous counter surfaces, and sufficient storage.		–	0	1
	9 Bedrooms All bedrooms in a Slow Home have good daylight, sufficient storage, a logical place for the bed, and enough room for circulation.		–	0	1
	10 Bathrooms All bathrooms in a Slow Home have private but accessible locations, are well-organized, modestly sized, and have sufficient counter space and storage.		–	0	1
	11 Utility A Slow Home has utility spaces for parking, laundry, mechanical equipment, and storage that are unobtrusively located, highly functional, and do not conflict with other uses.		–	0	1
	12 Organization A Slow Home is efficiently organized with like rooms grouped together and clear unobstructed circulation.		–	0	3

Minimum Design Quality Threshold *

0 - 6	7 - 12	13 - 16	17 - 20
Fast	Moderately Fast	Moderately Slow	Slow

n/a /20   8 /20   20 /20 ✓

Score   **Score**   **Score**

The Slow Home Test evaluates how well a property conforms to the Slow Home Philosophy of being simple to live in and light on the environment. Plot your score on the bar graph and refer to the summary on the reverse page to interpret your results.
* Properties that score below the Minimum Design Quality Threshold (13/20) don't sufficiently conform to the Slow Home philosophy and are not very simple or light places in which to live.

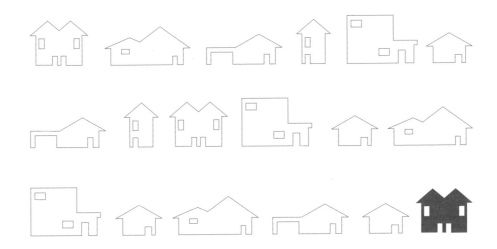

The Story of Gregor & Nancy

FROM FAST TO SLOW

The first step in the pursuit of a simpler and lighter way of life is to avoid fast houses in favor of Slow Homes. The apartment/loft that Luisa and Clara set out to purchase was a clear example of a Slow Home. Tom and Sarah's single-family house, on the other hand, was an unambiguous example of a fast house. But these two houses are just the two ends of a continuum of design quality. Most houses fall in between these two extremes. Some aspects of their design may be quite good, while others will be quite bad. What should be made of these properties that sit in between the perfect and the pitiful?

For new homes, the answer is straightforward. Any house earning a score of less than 13/20 on the Slow Home Test fails to meet the minimum design quality threshold and should not usually be considered for purchase. These residences have many more problems than they have assets in terms of design quality. As we learned from Tom and Sarah's experiences, this can lead to problems in both the short and long term.

Properties with a score of 17/20 or higher on the Test are considered Slow Homes. Any new home with a score in this range should be given the highest consideration for purchase.

The fate of a new home with a score of between 13/20 and 16/20 on the Test is not as straightforward. It usually requires more investigation to determine if it's appropriate for you or not. We call properties in this range Moderately Slow Homes, and although they are by no means perfect, many can still be effective places in which to live. Care definitely does need to be taken, however, to ensure that the specific design problems in the house under consideration are not significant impediments to the way you want to live.

Some people may not be all that concerned if the Test identifies a design problem in one particular area of the house. For other people, these deficiencies may be critical, and the property should be avoided. Consideration also needs to be given to any problems identified in the house-in-the-world section, as these environmental issues are more systemic and cannot as easily be changed by either current or future owners. While a new home in the moderately slow range should certainly be considered for purchase, it's important to proceed with a degree of caution and investigate the specifics of any potential design issue more fully before making any decisions.

THE SLOW HOME TEST
Evaluate the Quality of the Design Underlying Any House

Understanding Your Score

FAST HOUSE   (Score: 0 - 6)

If the property has a test score between 0 and 6, it's a fast house. 10% of North American residences have a score in this range.[†] These properties are badly designed with significant flaws throughout almost every part of the house. They will most likely be very difficult to live in and have a very high environmental footprint. Purchasing a property with a score in this range is not recommended. If this a residence you already own, caution is advised before undertaking any kind of remodeling. In most cases, not even a substantial project will be enough to fix the severity of the problems found in a fast house.

MODERATELY FAST HOUSE   (Score: 7 - 12)

If the property has a score between 7 and 12, it's a marginally fast house. 47% of North American residences have a score in this range.[†] These houses have more poor design features than good ones. As a result they're not very simple to live in or light on the environment. However, they can often be gems in the rough if you're willing and able to undertake a major remodeling project. Whether this is a residence you're considering to purchase, or one you already own, it's important to proceed carefully and fully investigate the potential costs and benefits of making the necessary improvements.

MODERATELY SLOW HOME   (Score: 13 - 16)

If the property has a score between 13 and 16, it's a marginally Slow Home. 32% of North American residences have a score in this range.[†] These properties have a good underlying design and there are problems in only a few areas. They're already quite simple and light places in which to live. However, a minor remodel can often upgrade them to a Slow Home. If this is a property that is currently listed for sale, it should be given very serious consideration. If it's a house you own, congratulations, you already live in a well designed residence that, with a few small improvements, could become really great.

SLOW HOME   (Score: 17 - 20)

If the property has a score between 17 and 20, it's a Slow Home. Only 11% of North American residences have a score in this range.[†] Its underlying design conforms to almost all of the Slow Home criteria for a high quality of life. Very little if anything needs to be done to improve the design and any improvements are probably relatively minor and easy to complete. Whether this is a property you already own or one that you are considering to buy, you should feel confident knowing that this is a great home that is simple to live in and light on the environment.

[†] Based on the results of the *2010 Slow Home Report on Design Quality in the North American New Home Market*, Calgary: Slow Home Studio, 2011.

The situation for resale homes is slightly more complicated but, at the same time, more promising. First, it's important to remember that fast houses are not a new phenomenon. The mass production housing industry has been building cookie-cutter houses for the past 60 years. The majority of this housing stock was originally designed-to-be-sold (rather than designed to be lived in), and we are just as liable to find a poorly designed fast house in a 1960s neighborhood as we are in a community that's currently being built on the fringe of the city. Even well-designed older homes are not immune to difficulties, as changing expectations for amenities and lifestyle can render parts of their original design obsolete.

Fortunately, with an older resale home, many of these problems can be overcome. The interior finishes and fixtures in a typical North American house are usually replaced, or at least upgraded, every 20 years. From a financial perspective, the interior is said to have reached the end of its economic life over that time and it becomes financially feasible for a homeowner to contemplate a major upgrade or remodel.

This is the moment of opportunity in the quest for a Slow Home. Reconfiguring an existing older house to make it simple to live in is an excellent way to create your own Slow Home.

Before we get into the details of how that works, it's important to review the three design criteria—location, size, and stewardship—in which older properties typically score much higher than their newer cousins. In fact, existing properties are often the most reasonable and most cost-effective source of homes that score well in the house-in-the-world section of the Slow Home Test.

Cities tend to grow in rings, like a tree, and communities that were developed decades ago are naturally going to be closer to the center than more recent subdivisions. Most large metropolitan areas actually have multiple centers, each with its own set of ringed development, so living "closer in" doesn't necessarily mean that the house has to be directly adjacent to downtown.

When chosen carefully, living in one of these older rings of development can bring you closer to where you work, shop, and play. This can have a significant impact on the amount of time you spend commuting in a car. Many of these neighborhoods are also better-connected to the mass transit system and have more community services and local retail than newer, more far-flung, communities. This makes them more walkable. As a result, an existing older property tends to meet the Slow Home criteria for a good location much more readily than a home in a new neighborhood. This is particularly true of single-family houses, since it's still relatively rare to find developments of new houses being built in existing communities. The chance of finding a new apartment/loft or townhouse project in an older neighborhood is much greater, as developers are more comfortable with the idea of replacing a tract of old houses with a higher-density project. Unfortunately, many of these are fast house developments, which are still beset with the usual list of fundamental design problems.

A reasonable house size is the second favorable design characteristic that's generally found in older properties. The floor area of our homes has expanded dramatically over the past 60 years as the fast house focus on quantity over quality took root in our collective consciousness. As with almost everything else in our world, we've been convinced that more is always better when it comes to house size. We live in a discount culture, where the price on the box is often more important than the quality of what's inside. In the housing market, where prices are usually compared in "per square foot" terms, simple economics dictates that the larger a house becomes, the more appealing it will seem to be.

Fortunately, the slow philosophy is beginning to change those expectations in terms of everything we purchase, from food, travel, and medicine, to the houses in which we live. While it will probably take some time, and a good deal of consumer pressure, to convince the fast house industry to reduce the size of the new houses it's building, the good news is that we can find these smaller houses right now, in older communities.

In most cities, there's a direct correlation between the age of a house and its size. Starting with the first mass-produced suburbs from the post World War II era, the typical three-bedroom house is a bungalow of about 900 square feet. Move out a few miles to a 1960s neighborhood, and the typical three-bedroom bungalow is closer to 1200 square feet. A little farther out and a decade later, and an 1500 square foot split-level is the prevailing house type. In a 1990s neighborhood, constructed just as the designed-to-be-sold marketing techniques of the fast house industry really started to take off, that same three-bedroom house is now two-storeys and closer to 2000 square feet. By comparison, all of these older properties are considerably smaller than the current average of 2300 square feet for a new single-family house.[14]

---

14   http://www.census.gov/const/C25Ann/sftotalmedavgsqft.pdf, Accessed Feb. 2011.

To be light on the environment, we all need to moderate the size of our houses and ensure that they are scaled more appropriately to our needs. A modestly sized house takes up less land, uses fewer materials to build, requires less energy to heat and cool, generates fewer greenhouse gases, and naturally limits the amount of other superfluous stuff in our lives. Living in an older home is a natural and effective strategy to achieve these environmental goals.

Finally, there is the issue of stewardship. As we know from the previous chapter, a house that's light on the environment needs to be worthy of the land on which it is sited, the materials embodied in its construction, and the energy expended in its daily operation. Designers and homeowners alike have an obligation to ensure that this environmental investment is well looked after for future generations. Choosing to live in an older house rather than a brand new one is an effective way to accomplish this, because it involves taking care of something that already exists, rather than causing something new to be created. It extends the useful life of the energy that was originally embodied in the construction of the house, and reuses the existing system of streets, utilities and public infrastructure. Making the commitment to an older community also brings new life to the area and extends its social well-being.

The closer location, modest size, and extended service life of an existing house makes it an excellent choice for lightening your impact on the environment.

AVERAGE HOUSE SIZE BY DECADE

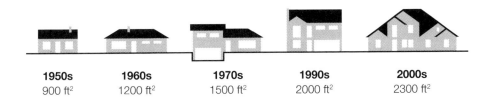

1950s	1960s	1970s	1990s	2000s
900 ft²	1200 ft²	1500 ft²	2000 ft²	2300 ft²

When considered in their original state, however, most of these older homes are not necessarily simple to live in. Many are fast houses that were, in their day, also designed-to-be-sold. Others may have been well-designed for their time but are now obsolete, unable to adapt effectively to the specific demands of our busy 21st century lives. These problems include too few closets, not enough bathrooms, poor back entry spaces, enclosed kitchens with limited workspace or storage, and living spaces that have little-to-no connection with the outdoors.

Fortunately, most, if not all, of these problems can be fixed with some sort of remodel. Reconfiguring an existing older house to make it simple to live in is an excellent and cost-effective way to own a Slow Home. It combines the inherent environmental advantages of a good location, a modest size, and effective stewardship with all of the functional requirements of a house that fits the way you really want to live. The one proviso to this good news is that most older homes require exterior upgrades to the windows and insulation in order to improve thermal performance, as well as technical upgrades to the mechanical, plumbing, and electrical systems. These are typically easy to accomplish in any major remodeling project.

The end result is that the large numbers of older properties that achieve only a moderate score on the Slow Home Test (7/20 - 16/20) may not be problems as much as opportunities. They are diamonds in the rough, awaiting a second round of design intervention that will bring them to their full Slow Home potential. Of course, not all properties are good candidates for this kind of reuse. Some are in poor physical condition, which precludes remodeling, while others just have too many problems that can't be fixed. Other properties are on sites that should more appropriately be redeveloped to a higher density house type, while others may have had more recent "fast remodeling" changes that make them too expensive for a major project to be economically feasible at this point.

Generally speaking, however, any older house with a high score in the house-in-the-world section of the Slow Home Test should be seriously investigated as a candidate for a substantial remodeling project. In many situations, and for many people, it's the best and most feasible option for living in a Slow Home.

IN PRAISE OF OLDER HOMES

I first met Gregor and Nancy when they came to our office for assistance in looking for a new home. This recently retired couple was planning to relocate to our city in order to be closer to their daughter and her family. Gregor and Nancy were fortunate. They had sold their large family home five years before we met, well before the financial crisis, and had been living in a rental house in their old neighborhood as they finished off their jobs and tried to figure out what they wanted to do with the next phase of their lives. They were now in a good position to fulfill their retirement dream of a small townhouse located near their daughter.

After an initial meeting to discuss the sorts of things they were looking for in their new house, I had arranged to take them on a preliminary tour of potential properties. This had not gone particularly well. The couple was now back in my office ready for their second tour.

"You'd better have something good for us today, John," Gregor said, with his usual gruffness. The truth was that I thought I had indeed found a great property for them, although I also anticipated that it would take some convincing for Gregor to see it that way.

At our first meeting, I had been told in no uncertain terms that they were only interested in new townhouse projects.

"Gregor doesn't want to have to worry about maintenance issues," Nancy informed me. "In our old home, they took too much time away from his sports."

However, on the first property tour, Gregor had complained about the location of all of the new townhouse projects as well as their shoddy construction. He also thought they were overpriced. On these three issues, at least, we could agree.

"Gregor, today I have another option that I think takes care of the concerns you had with the first set of homes we looked at."

"That's exciting," Nancy said, as a flash of relief crossed her face. "See, Gregor, I told you this wouldn't be a waste of time."

It was at this point that Matthew walked in. After some brief introductions, I explained what the couple hoped to find.

"Basically, we're looking for an open-plan living space with a good kitchen because Nancy likes to cook. They also have a large dining table for the weekly dinners they plan to have with their daughter's family. Also, Gregor likes to watch sports on his large TV. Nancy thinks he would enjoy having a separate room for that and some of his other things."

Gregor nodded slowly.

Glancing at Nancy, Matthew replied, "I can see why that would be a good thing."

"Other than that, they'd like a master bedroom with a nice en-suite bathroom and a second bedroom and bathroom for occasional guests. I understand that Gregor's brother comes to stay with them for several weeks at a time," I concluded.

"He likes to watch the sports, too," Nancy said absently.

Gregor leaned back with a big grin. "Plus we want something good—a house that lasts, like in the old country. But not too expensive!"

With more than a little apprehension, I suggested that we all go and look at the property I had found.

The townhouse I was going to show them was a 1370 square foot two storey end unit. There were two bedrooms, two and a half baths, and a single car garage in the under-drive basement. It was located in a great older neighborhood with shops, a public library, and a park within easy walking distance. There was a bus stop at the end of the street and their daughter's house was only about five miles away.

The townhouse was also 35 years old and the interior had never been updated.

"What's this all about?" Gregor asked as we pulled up to the address. "Are they ripping these down?"

"Not exactly," I said. "Most of the units in this development are in great shape and worth a lot of money. But don't say anything more until we go in and have a look."

Both Gregor and Nancy looked a bit skeptical as I opened the front door.

The front entry was dark and a little cramped. In fact, there wasn't really enough room for all of us to enter the house at the same time. I noted that there was a small closet and guest bathroom to the right of the entrance as I led the way down the long hallway that extended from the front door to the back of the unit. Along the way, we passed a small formal dining room and kitchen on the left and what looked like a study on the right. So far, the interior of the townhouse was dark and more than a little depressing. It also smelled its age.

Nancy and Matthew stopped off in the kitchen while Gregor and I continued into the living room. This was a more pleasant space with sunlight streaming in through the south-facing patio doors. The furniture was oddly placed in the room, however, making it feel smaller than it really was.

"Funny joke," Gregor said, turning around. "Let's get out of here and go see the real house. This place gives me the creeps." I was just about to respond when Matthew and Nancy emerged from their exploration of the kitchen.

"What a great house," Matthew exclaimed. "You've gotta check out the kitchen. There's a kitchen table on one side of the door and a big dining table on the other. Talk about redundant spaces!"

Seeing the look on Gregor's face, Nancy quickly jumped in. "Matthew told me we have to look beyond what's here right now, dear. The insides of this house are all worn out and need to be replaced. But that doesn't matter. It means we can change it all around. It could be just the way you want it."

Sensing a bit of a reprieve, I suggested that we tour the rest of the house. The basement was basic, with an oversized single-car garage, a mechanical room, and some storage space. Upstairs, the two bedrooms were generously sized and had good windows that let in lots of light.

"You need to look past the green shag carpeting," I suggested, as Gregor shook his head in disbelief. "These rooms have great bones."

GREGOR & NANCY`S TOWNHOUSE

Dining
Room

Kitchen

Living
Room

Terrace

Front
Entry

Study

UP

DN

Main Floor
Interior - 690 ft²

Master
En-suite

Master
Bedroom

Deck

Bathroom

Laundry

Bedroom
2

DN

Upper Floor
Interior - 680 ft²
Deck - 25 ft²

The same could not be said of the bathrooms. They were in bad shape. Aside from the pink fixtures, the tired cabinetry, and even more shag carpeting, the layouts were all wrong. The master bathroom sink cabinet was located in a small alcove that opened directly into the master bedroom. The direct view of this vanity from the bed was less than ideal. Beyond the sink, there was an enclosed room containing the toilet and bathtub. Here, at least, there was tile.

I accompanied Gregor to the second bathroom, which was no better than the first. It had an awkward non-standard layout with a small shower in the corner. There were no drawers in the sink cabinet.

Nancy and Matthew had already returned to the main floor. I suggested to Gregor that we join them as he told me in no uncertain terms that he was questioning my continued involvement in this process. We congregated at the kitchen counter and I opened my folder to retrieve a completed Slow Home Test.

"Gregor, I appreciate your patience," I began. "As you have pointed out, this house has a lot of problems. I completed a Slow Home Test on the property and, as you can see, it only scored 1/10 in the house-as-a-whole section."

Matthew looked a little surprised at my generosity, but I countered, "I gave it the single point for the utility spaces because I liked the laundry room as well as the attached under-drive single car garage."

"I don't need some piece of paper to tell me that this house is all wrong," Gregor said, with more than a bit of frustration in his voice.

"Perhaps not, but let's look at the other half of the Test. In the house-in-the-world section, this house scored a perfect 10/10. It has a great walkable location, it's modestly sized, and it's oriented to the south. It also scores well in stewardship because it's an older house in an established neighborhood. You remember that none of the new townhouse projects we looked at last time had environmental scores that were anywhere near this good."

Gregor nodded as Nancy squeezed his hand affectionately. "But that's still only 11/20," he said. "That means it's one of those, what do you call them, fast houses, right?"

Matthew jumped in. "For the moment, yes. But when I look at this house, I see potential, not problems. Almost all of the issues with the way the interior of the property currently works can be fixed with a remodel. The basics are sound. We can change the rest."

I retrieved a floor plan from my folder and placed it on the counter. I had seen the potential to turn this fast house into a great Slow Home when I had visited the property on my own a few days earlier. Knowing that Gregor would not be as easily convinced, I had sketched out the existing floor plan as a base on which to draw out what this house could be in the future. Slowly, Matthew and I explained our ideas to Nancy and Gregor.

REVISING THE MAIN FLOOR

I started the discussion by reviewing all of the shortcomings with the floor plan. This can be an effective strategy after doing a walkthrough inspection, because floor plans offer a different perspective. In many ways, they're like x-rays and help you see below the surface to better understand what's really going on. As with x-rays, floor plans can also help you diagnose the true source of a problem. For example, an x-ray can tell you that a pain in your foot is actually being caused by an old injury to your back. In the same way, a floor plan can reveal that the problem in one room is actually the result of a bad design decision made somewhere else in the house.

"Notice how the location of the fireplace disrupts the living room," I said. "It's too close to the windows and that creates havoc with the furniture placement. The fireplace is a natural focal point, around which the furniture is usually organized. Having it so close to the wall results in the furniture being too close to the end wall. That restricts access to the patio doors and leaves a lot of wasted space in the room. The result is a room that feels smaller than it really is."

Both Gregor and Nancy nodded.

Matthew continued. "The kitchen has a different problem. It has a fairly big floor area but the proportions are all wrong. The result is a lack of counter space and storage, to say nothing of a bad work triangle between the appliances."

MAIN FLOOR ANALYSIS

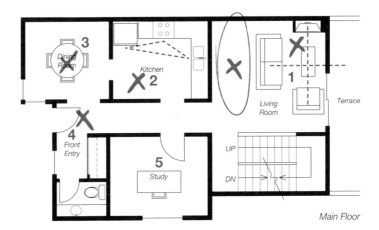

Main Floor

1. *The fireplace location restricts furniture layout and results in wasted space adjacent to the kitchen.*

2. *The kitchen is enclosed, has a poor work triangle, too much floor space, and no natural light.*

3. *The dining room is in an enclosed space separate from the living area.*

4. *The front entry is narrow and cramped.*

5. *The study has good potential but the current desk placement is awkward.*

This kind of layout was actually quite common in older houses because they were intended to accommodate a small kitchen table. This practice has all but disappeared in recent times, usually resulting in a large empty space in one corner of the kitchen, similar to the one found in this townhouse.

"On the other hand, the formal dining room actually works well," Matthew said. "It's a good size and proportion and could easily fit your table. My concern is that it's too separate from the rest of the house. It kind of disappears when you're not using it. Combining this space with the living room would increase the apparent size of the house."

"I see what you mean," Nancy said. "We only use the dining table in the evenings for dinner. I guess that's a bit of a waste."

"It's not that you need to actually use the table more often, but it would be nice to be able to feel that space throughout the day," I concluded.

The front entry was also an issue. Although the guest bath was well located and the front closet was a good size, the floor area devoted to entry was just too small. Plus, the long hallway to the main living spaces was tight and dark. This was an area that would also need some serious attention.

"To end on a good note, we have the study," I said, "Right now, as we saw, it just has a single desk in the middle of the room. That's not an effective use of the space. I think there's a lot of potential there."

"So, what do you boys think should be done to improve this house?" Gregor asked, with a combination of sarcasm and curiosity in his voice.

"Let's start by looking at the overall organization," I said. "We can see from the existing floor plan that it's actually quite clearly organized into two long zones of use, with an area for circulation in the center. In this context, the location of the staircase makes sense. It's unobtrusive but easily accessible. That's why I said this unit had good bones. The problem right now is that each of the two long zones has been broken up into a series of individual rooms. While this is effective on the one side to accommodate the guest bathroom and study, the other side doesn't need to be so closed in. If we remove those walls and open it up to include the hallway, the main floor of this house will feel much bigger and more open."

"Let's imagine starting with a clean slate on that side of the house," I said, as I redrew the plan with the walls removed.

"That looks better already. Maybe we should just leave it at that and move in," Nancy joked.

"Our goal is to add the kitchen, dining and living rooms while still maintaining that open space feel," I said. "To do that, we need to relocate the kitchen to the front of the house."

Kitchens are generally most successful when placed in a corner, looking out into the rest of the house. I drew counters around all three sides of the new kitchen and added a peninsula

REVISING THE MAIN FLOOR

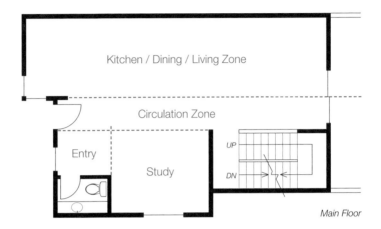

Main Floor

that faced the main living space. I then placed one appliance on each of the three sides. "This kitchen will work much better. It also makes good use of the existing window at the front."

"Notice how the appliance triangle is efficient and located at the back of the kitchen," Matthew added. "This means that the area around the peninsula is out of the primary cooking zone and is left open for preparation as well as social seating."

"That's really nice," Nancy said. "Everybody always likes to congregate in the kitchen. With this layout, they won't be getting in my way."

Gregor grunted what I assumed was a small bit of approval.

"This design also means that the long hallway has been eliminated. That floor area is now part of the main living space. The short piece of wall that remains by the kitchen defines the entry space, but after that, it's all open," I continued.

The next step was to draw in the revised living room. I had already removed the original fireplace from the drawing and now started to insert a new fireplace, situated a little further down the wall. I left some space for the fireplace ducting to the right of the hearth and

DRAWING THE KITCHEN LIVING AND DINING ROOMS

Main Floor

1   The fireplace is relocated to better accommodate a furniture grouping without obstructing the dining area.

2   The dining table is centered between the kitchen and living area with sufficient space for circulation.

3   The kitchen is relocated to the front of the unit with an effective appliance triangle, plenty of work surfaces, storage space, and a peninsula eating bar.

balanced it with a bookcase on the left. I also made sure to allow enough room for the dining table by the kitchen.

"The key to a good living room is an effective focal point," Matthew said as he began to draw on the floor plan. "Notice how we can now center the furniture layout on John's new fireplace in a way that eliminates all the wasted space and awkward circulation in the old plan. It also means we have a clear circulation route out to the back terrace."

Matthew finished off this part of the plan by drawing the dining table in the space between the kitchen and the living room. The new configuration provided plenty of space around the table without conflicting with either the bar stools at the peninsula or the living room furniture.

Shifting everyone's attention to the study, I looked directly at Gregor. "I know you need a quiet place to work and watch TV. We can make this space great for both of those uses.

DRAWING THE ENTRY AND STUDY

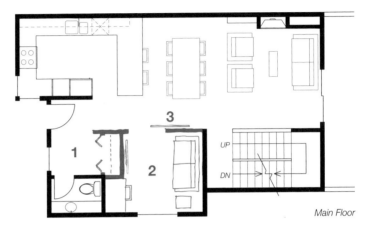

Main Floor

1   *Coat closet relocated to expand floor area for the front entry.*

2   *Sofa situated in front of tv with corner study desk adjacent to the window.*

3   *Barn door added to create privacy for study / tv room.*

The first step is to move and enlarge the doorway so there's a better connection with the main space and enough room to place a long sofa along the back wall. Now, let's create a niche by the window for your desk and put in bookcases above it for all of your stuff. We can mount your flat screen TV on the wall right in front of the sofa. It's a perfect distance away for watching sports. If we add a sliding barn door on the outside of the space, you can close off this room when you're watching TV but, when you're not, it can be left open to the rest of the house."

Gregor started to nod and Nancy looked pleased. "I've always wanted Gregor's TV to have its own space," she mused.

I had suggested the niche for Gregor's desk because it also allowed me to relocate the front closet into that part of the floor plan without it causing any obstructions. The result I was looking for was more room in the entry. "Notice how the front entry is no longer a narrow hallway with an alcove for the closet, but one larger single space that extends from the kitchen to the guest bathroom."

Nancy looked at the finished plan. "I can't believe it," she said. "It's almost as if you added more space! When we first walked in here, all I could think about was how small and dingy this place was. But with this plan, I can see that we could have lots of room. "

"Maybe," Gregor said. "Let's see what you can do upstairs."

REVISING THE UPPER FLOOR

Having made it past the first hurdle with at least some level of acceptance from Gregor, I brought out my drawing of the existing second floor.

Once again, I began by reviewing the problems with the existing layout. "The guest bedroom is a good size but I think the door location and closet access are awkward. That area feels like an add-on to the room. The bathroom for that room has more problems. It's tight and there's almost no storage. I know that may not be a big deal when it's being used by guests, but when you sell the house it could end up being used as a regular bedroom. In that case, I think we need to have at least one set of drawers by the sink."

"I agree," said Nancy. "Gregor renovated the bathroom in our old house and reduced the size of the vanity to make room for the Finnish sauna he wanted to have. The realtor said he had a devil of a time selling it."

Moving on to the master bedroom, Matthew added, "This room is huge, but not in a good way. I like the window and the little outside deck, but the other end of the room is too long. There's also almost no closet space. Looking at the master bathroom, I think the best thing to say is that we just need to start over."

"In terms of overall organization, I think we can keep everything in the same basic location," I said as I redrew the second floor plan. "In remodeling projects like this, you typically want to try and move as few walls as possible on the second floor. Let's tackle the guest bedroom first."

UPPER FLOOR ANALYSIS

Upper Floor

1   Bathroom is too small and has no storage beside the sink.

2   Door swing to bedroom 2 conflicts with closet access.

3   Master bedroom is awkwardly shaped with too much floor area.

4   Master closet is too small.

5   Master en-suite vanity is open to the master bedroom.

I reconfigured the location of the bedroom door in order to remove the awkward space at the end of the room. By relocating the closet, I created an open area adjacent to the stair that was a perfect size for the laundry.

"I know I said I liked the laundry space when we were reviewing the Slow Home Test results, but I like this one just as much. The main reason for moving the laundry to this part of the plan is that it creates more room for the bathrooms to change," I said.

"Okay by me," said Gregor. His wife smiled.

Pen in hand, Matthew continued with the redesign of the master bedroom.

'The goal is to create a well-proportioned room," he said. "That means extending the wall of the closet all the way to the end of the room."

DRAWING THE BEDROOMS AND LAUNDRY

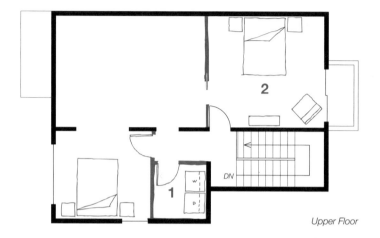

Upper Floor

1   *Laundry room relocated to provide more space for bathrooms. Machines placed away from bedroom wall.*

2   *Master bedroom is more appropriately sized with shared access door to closet and en-suite bathroom.*

The resulting bedroom looked much better. The readjustment had corrected the room's proportions and the bed could now be centered on the back wall and still be close to the window. There was even enough room to add a small chair in the corner. This would be a nice, sunlit place for Nancy to sit and read when she needed some time on her own.

All of the second floor changes that had been done so far had left a large, rectangular open space in the front corner of the plan. Matthew now set about to apportion this area into two bathrooms and closets. "I think the best strategy is to have the guest bathroom run along the length of the front wall. This will only take up a little more than five feet of space and it still leaves a large rectangular area for the master en-suite."

Matthew's next move was to add a large walk-in closet adjacent to the master bedroom, which opened out to a large vanity. The result was a variation on the original layout that separated the bathroom sink from the rest of the plumbing fixtures. This time, however, the

DRAWING THE BATHROOMS

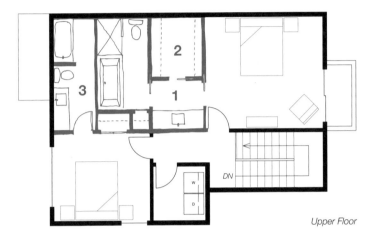

Upper Floor

1   Segmented master en-suite layout creates separate area for sink and vanity with good counter space and storage.

2   Master walk-in closet is appropriately sized and accessed through sink area.

3   Second bathroom has efficient layout with good counter space and storage.

vanity was also in its own space, distinct from the bedroom and connected to the closet. He concluded the design by sketching in the toilet, bathtub and stand-alone shower in the space adjacent to the guest bathroom.

This layout had several advantages. The first was that there was only one door in the bedroom that led to both the bathroom and the closet. This would allow easy access between the bathroom and the closet without having to go back into the bedroom. As a result, Gregor would be able to get ready in the morning without causing a disturbance on those fortunate days when Nancy was able to sleep in. The segmented bathroom arrangement also allowed one person to use the sink area while the second used the other facilities.

"I see you were able to sneak the guest bedroom closet into the space beside the master bathtub. Very clever," Nancy added.

Having completed our presentation of the floor plans, we steeled ourselves for the moment of truth. I asked Gregor what he thought of our ideas.

After a long pause, he said quietly, "I think this will work. You boys did a good job. But before we get too carried away, what about costs? I'm not made of money, you know."

Smiling, I began to describe the economic model behind the transformation of a fast house into a Slow Home.

In a conventional real estate transaction, the entire housing budget is usually spent on the purchase of a property. The result can be a long and difficult search, particularly when the goal is finding a Slow Home. At the other end of the spectrum is the option of buying an existing property, removing the old house, and building a new one. In this case, the maximum amount of money that can be spent on the purchase of the property is determined by subtracting the estimated construction costs from the overall housing budget. The obvious advantage of this approach is that the new house can be designed properly from scratch. The challenge is that high land costs often limit the feasibility of the project for modest housing budgets.

Fortunately, the idea of distributing a housing budget over a combination of property purchase and construction need not be restricted to the construction of newly built homes. It can also be applied to a remodeling project in which an older fast house or moderately slow home is purchased and then reconstructed into a Slow Home. The key is to factor the cost of the remodel into the purchase price for the property and integrate an allowance for the construction costs into the housing budget from the start of the project. This means that the target purchase price for the property is the overall housing budget less the anticipated cost of the improvements.

With the right property selection, an existing fast house can be transformed according to the Slow Home principles into a home that's simple to live in and light on the environment. The reduced construction cost of remodeling rather than building new means that this type of project is feasible for a much wider range of housing budgets. In fact, in our experience, this model can be used for almost any housing budget.

GREGOR & NANCY`S COMPLETED DESIGN

Kitchen

Dining Room

Living Room

Terrace

Front Entry

Study / TV

N E S W

Main Floor

Bathroom

Walk-in Closet

Master En-suite

Master Bedroom

Deck

Bedroom 2

Laundry

W D

Upper Floor

Based on previous townhouse remodeling projects that we had completed, Matthew and I had a pretty good idea of how much money Gregor and Nancy would need to transform the interior of a modestly sized townhouse. Subtracting that figure from their housing budget gave us the price range for the property search. The property I had selected for them fit within this range.

"Gregor, the purchase price of this townhouse is about two thirds of your overall housing budget," I said. "Based on the concept plans that we've discussed today, Matthew and I believe that the remodeling work can be done for a little less than the remaining third."

Matthew elaborated. "We need to do a preliminary estimate to confirm a few prices, but my sense is that this budget will be sufficient to undertake all of the work we have discussed so far."

"That's an interesting way of thinking about real estate," Gregor admitted, as he started to warm to the idea. "It's like in Europe, where we build new buildings on top of old ones. Rather than starting a building project with a bare piece of land, we start with an existing structure."

SLOW HOME BUDGET DISTRIBUTION

Total Budget

30% of Budget Spent on Improvements

100% of Budget Spent on Property

Target Property Purchase

70% of Budget Spent on Property

TYPICAL
REAL ESTATE TRANSACTION

SLOW HOME
REAL ESTATE TRANSACTION

"Exactly, and if you can find the right piece of property, it can also make great environmental sense because you're reusing the embodied energy in the materials that made up the original house," Matthew said.

Gregor nodded, with the hint of a smile. "I think this looks very promising."

The next step for Gregor and Nancy was to secure the land with a purchase contract that was conditional on a satisfactory architectural review. This allowed two weeks for Matthew and me to draw up the concept design in more detail and develop a preliminary cost estimate.

Gregor and Nancy were pleased with the refined floor plans, and the construction estimate was within their budget. They decided to release the condition and proceed with the project. We worked on the design for another two months and began construction just after the couple took possession of the property. They moved into their Slow Home about five months later.

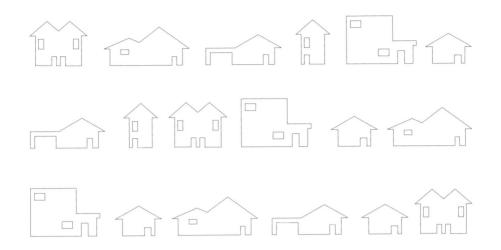

The Bigger Picture

A NATIONAL SURVEY OF DESIGN QUALITY

Until recently, it probably didn't matter much whether or not people like Tom and Sarah, Luisa and Clara, or Gregor and Nancy could tell the difference between a fast house and a Slow Home. If they didn't like their current house, they would simply have moved to a new one. In fact, too many of us had become accustomed to trying to solve our "what's wrong with this house" problems by regularly trading up to ever-bigger and more expensive homes.

That the same problems seemed to keep reappearing in each house we purchased was just a minor annoyance. The promise of the next dream house, and a big jump in personal net worth, was always just around the corner.

For better or worse, those days are gone. The severity of the housing market's recent collapse means that the easy mobility we enjoyed through 60 years of steadily increasing house values and a seemingly endless pool of homebuyers has all but disappeared. Decades of built-up equity have been erased and the financial ladder of home ownership has been destabilized. An alarming number of people are trapped by mortgages that exceed their home's current value. The resale market is choked with foreclosed properties that refuse to sell, and the new home industry is virtually dormant in many areas. Current predictions are that it will take years, if not decades, for the real estate market to correct itself.[15]

Gone are the days of recklessly trading in one fast house for another. Suddenly, in the face of a future in which many of us will be living in our houses for much longer periods of time, the design quality of those homes becomes a much more top-of-mind issue than their speculative value as financial investments.

It's also important to remember that the house as an investment vehicle is a relatively recent phenomenon. Prior to the 1950s, houses were simply another consumer durable like a car or a suit of clothes. The price we paid for them returned a dividend in terms of utility rather than equity. In other words, the definition of a good home was one that was a good place in which to live. By and large, the housing industry of the time delivered on that promise with generations of simple, modest, well-designed homes.

---

15   Edward L. Glasser, *Why Your House's Value (Probably) Won't Rise*, The New York Times, April 6, 2010

The idea that houses could also be an investment first arose with post-war America's residential construction boom; house prices began to consistently climb faster than the rate of inflation. It has only been in the last 20 years, however, that the differential became great enough that houses became a serious investment opportunity. During that period, property speculation took hold of our collective imagination and many of us began to regard our houses as magical ATM machines filled with ready cash. Although houses had been solid investments for several decades, the idea that a successful home was primarily a good place to live was almost completely eclipsed by its potential as a clever financial strategy. Is it any wonder that, as the housing industry worked to deliver on this promise, the designed-to-be-sold attitude took hold so strongly?

We are at the dawn of a new reality in residential real estate. As the economic panic of the past two years starts to subside and we become more accustomed to a world where houses are not, first and foremost at least, investment vehicles, we need to realize that the truest, and perhaps only, real value in our homes lies in their ability to provide us with a great place in which to live.

At the same time, we need to finally accept that reducing our home's environmental footprint is no longer just an option, but a firm obligation that each of us has to make. In light of this "new normal" in the housing market, it begins to matter a great deal if the house we live in, or the one that we may be considering for purchase, is a fast house, a Slow Home, or something in between.

Within this context, the question "what's wrong with this house?" becomes an important one for each of us to ask. Unfortunately, for many people, the answers will probably not be encouraging. The badly designed houses in the stories of Tom and Sarah, Luisa and Clara, and Gregor and Nancy are not isolated instances but form part of a much larger trend of poor design quality that runs throughout the North American housing market.

To better understand this broader context, Matthew and I recently completed a nine-month research project that undertook the first survey of design quality in the North American housing industry. We enlisted the help of more than 100 volunteers from across Canada and the United States to participate in a mass collaboration effort to identify and evaluate over 4,600 new residential projects in nine cities — Toronto, Philadelphia, Atlanta, Miami, Chicago,

DESIGN QUALITY BY CITY

Percent of Houses Analyzed Meeting the Minimum Design Quality Criteria

1	Vancouver	**64**%
2	Philadelphia	**56**%
3	Denver	**44**%
4	Chicago	**42**%
5	Los Angeles	**41**%
6	Toronto	**37**%
7	Atlanta	**37**%
8	Dallas	**35**%
9	Miami	**29**%

7 of the 9 cities surveyed received a failing grade in house design quality.

OVERALL DESIGN QUALITY

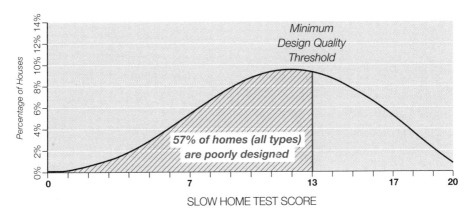

Dallas, Denver, Los Angeles, and Vancouver. This virtual community searched the web for new residential projects in three housing categories—apartment/lofts, townhomes, and single-family houses. They used the standardized Slow Home Test to evaluate the floor plans and then posted the results to our database. Matthew and I analyzed the results to both identify larger trends in the data and establish the most common design pitfalls.

The results, released in the *2010 Slow Home Report on Design Quality in the North American New Home Market*,[16] confirmed our worst suspicions. More than half (57 percent) of the more than 4,600 new home projects that were analyzed in our survey failed to achieve a score of 13/20 or greater on the Slow Home Test. This is what we consider to be the minimum design quality threshold, and properties that do not attain this score will be difficult to live in and hard on the environment. In our opinion, these fast houses are so poorly designed that they should not normally be considered for purchase.

The results were even more alarming when broken down by house type. More than three out of every four (78 percent) of the single-family houses surveyed failed to meet the minimum threshold. The level of design quality was slightly better for townhouses, with just over half (57 percent) failing to meet the minimum threshold for design quality. Interestingly, apartment/ lofts scored much better, with only 38 percent of projects receiving a failing grade.

OVERALL DESIGN QUALITY BY HOUSE TYPE

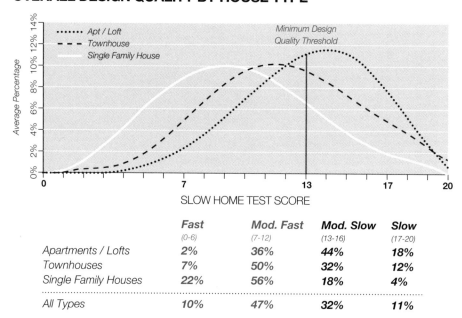

	Fast	Mod. Fast	Mod. Slow	Slow
	(0-6)	*(7-12)*	*(13-16)*	*(17-20)*
Apartments / Lofts	2%	36%	44%	18%
Townhouses	7%	50%	32%	12%
Single Family Houses	22%	56%	18%	4%
All Types	10%	47%	32%	11%

16   A digital copy of the report is available at www.slowhomestudio.com

On the other end of the scale, a mere 11 percent of properties in all house types achieved a score of 17/20 or greater to earn the classification of Slow Home. For single-family houses, the percentage of these exceptionally well-designed homes dropped to just 4 percent. For townhouses, the number was 12 percent, and apartment/lofts again fared the best, with 18 percent of the properties surveyed achieving top marks for design quality.

We attribute the higher level of design quality in the apartment/loft category to the fact that, unlike single-family houses and low-rise townhouse developments, many apartment/loft projects are large, multi-storey buildings that require the services of a professional architect for their design.

The level of design quality also varied substantially over the nine cities in the survey. Vancouver had the best overall level of design quality, with 64 percent of properties in all house types exceeding the minimum design quality threshold. Miami was the worst of the nine cities, with only 29 percent of the properties in all house types receiving a minimum pass or better on the Slow Home Test.

The most significant of our detailed findings was the identification of the four designed-to-be-sold strategies described in the chapter on Tom and Sarah's fast house. The first of these strategies was colliding geometries. They are employed to catch the attention of homebuyers when they first walk into a house, and were noted in 17 percent of all house types. Colliding geometries were most prevalent in single-family houses (32 percent).

Redundant spaces was the second designed-to-be-sold strategy and are used to ignite the homebuyer's desire by artificially inflating the allure of a home with extra rooms and functions. They were found in 23 percent of all of the properties in the survey. Most redundant spaces end up being rarely used because they don't function effectively. Multiple living and dining rooms were the most common example of redundant spaces across all house types.

The third strategy, false labeling, is also used to ignite desire in the homebuyer by giving evocative room names to deficient areas in the plan. The goal is to make a house look better in the sales brochure than it is in reality. False labeling was observed in 36 percent of all the properties surveyed. In single-family houses and townhouses, the most common falsely labeled spaces were foyers. In apartment/lofts, falsely labeled study/office spaces were the most prevalent.

Supersizing is the fourth and final designed-to-be-sold strategy that was identified in the survey. It was noted in 37 percent of all properties. The purpose of supersizing is to give the illusion of value by seducing the buyer with the offer of more "product" at a cut-rate price. Most of these over-scaled features and rooms are less functional, however, than a more reasonably sized version. The survey identified instances of supersizing ranging from individual elements, such as bathtubs and staircases, to oversized spaces such as garages, bathrooms and master bedrooms. The so-called "trophy kitchen" was a type of supersizing found almost exclusively in large single-family houses. The multiple islands and large floor areas typical in these kitchens often resulted in ineffective and awkward kitchen layouts. Oversized master bathrooms were the most prevalent forms of Supersizing across all housing types.

On the positive side, the survey found no correlation between design quality and price. This indicates that, contrary to popular belief, building a house that follows the fundamentals of good residential design does not necessarily translate into higher construction costs. The results suggest that for a given size range, finish level, and type of house, a well-designed Slow Home was about the same price as a poorly designed fast house. This means that the often-used excuse that good design is unaffordable to the average homeowner is no excuse at all. It merely masks a general lack of care and attention to the fundamentals of good design across the spectrum of house prices.

DESIGNED-TO-BE-SOLD PROBLEMS BY HOUSE TYPE

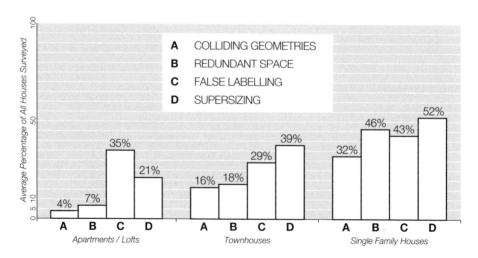

Finally, the survey revealed only a slight correlation between design quality and house size. This correlation was only found in the single-family house type, and only at the top end of the size range. The survey noted a drop in the already low level of design quality in large single-family houses (over 4,000 square feet). Interestingly, houses of this size are commonly called McMansions, supersized icons of overconsumption that represent the epitome of fast house thinking. It therefore comes as no surprise that their level of design quality was less than the norm.

THINK LIKE AN ARCHITECT

The survey results suggest that there is a deep crisis of design quality in the North American housing industry. There are far too many fast houses that have been designed-to-be-sold, and not enough Slow Homes that are well-designed, sustainable places in which to live. The homes in which we live are too important to our well-being, too large a financial investment, and have too big an environmental impact for this to continue.

Dolores Hayden, professor of Architecture and American Studies at Yale University, argues that "the personal happiness of many Americans has been undermined by poorly designed housing and public space, yet few of us employ the language of real estate development, architecture, or urban planning to trace the contours of loneliness, boredom, weariness, discrimination or financial worry in our lives." [17]

As an example, she describes how the frequent complaint that "there aren't enough hours in the day" to do all the things one has to do should more appropriately be described as the result of bad housing choices that result in the need for too much driving.

To that, I would add that instead of complaining that "my house is too small," it's more accurate, and more useful, to describe the specific design problems in your house that make the daily routines of life difficult and inhibit the way you want to live. Our inability to clearly articulate the problems with our houses severely limits our ability to solve them.

---

17   Dolores Hayden, *Redesigning the American Dream*, New York: WW Norton & Co, p. 58.

We, as home-owners and home-buyers, need to develop an understanding of design fundamentals that allows us to determine more precisely what's actually wrong, as well as what's right, with any house we may be considering. We need to learn how to look past the marketing glitz of the feature sheet and evaluate more fully the design quality of the house.

In short, we need to start thinking like architects rather than passive consumers.

This doesn't mean that we all need to go to architecture school. The Slow Food movement certainly doesn't advocate that we become professional chefs in order to take more control of the food we eat. Rather, the movement asks that we learn the basics of happy, healthy and socially responsible eating and how to apply these guidelines to our own lives.

In the same way that chefs like the U.K.'s Jamie Oliver offer easy rules and instructions that you can easily use in order to become "a bit more streetwise about cooking,"[18] the Slow Home design principles outlined in this book empower you to become a bit more streetwise about design and make more educated decisions about where and how you live.

This does not eliminate the need for professional advice. It's always good practice to consult with an architect or other design professional whenever you are making big decisions about your home. I also believe that an architectural design quality review should be part of the due diligence process in every real estate transaction, regardless of whether construction is planned or not. There are many times, however, when it's not really necessary to enlist the services of an architect. In these situations, a basic understanding of the Slow Home design principles will enable you to evaluate the design quality of a house on your own.

In the midst of the financial pain and suffering that this housing crisis has wrought on so many people, I believe we also have the seeds of change. In the same way that a pine forest needs a wildfire to cause new growth to sprout, the dramatic events of recent years have perhaps finally cleared the way for each of us to start making real, substantive changes in the way we think about our houses.

---

18   Jamie Oliver, *Jamie's Food Revolution*, New York: Hyperion, 2009, p.8.

For the many people who currently find that they are living in a fast house that doesn't meet their needs and can't be easily sold, Tom and Sarah's story demonstrates that "thinking like an architect" can help create a roadmap for modest change that offers the promise of a short-term solution during this period of economic recovery.

For those people who are in the market for a new or resale property, Luisa and Clara's story is a reminder that "thinking like an architect" can help you make smarter real estate choices that simplify the way you live and lighten your environmental impact.

Finally, the story of Gregor and Nancy speaks to how "thinking like an architect" can empower you to step outside of the fast housing industry and transform an existing property into a Slow Home. At a time when many people find themselves living in older fast houses, this strategy can apply just as much to a house you may currently own as it does to one that you are hoping to purchase.

I believe that everyone can, and should live, in a Slow Home – a place to live that makes our lives not only simpler and lighter, but also more meaningful and joyful. All it takes is the courage to honestly consider the design quality of our homes and, if necessary, chart a path towards change.

We all want to go home again. Perhaps now is the time for that journey to begin.